Addition.
The Litt
the Shrinking Dollar

"A financial catastrophe is approaching. How? When? No one knows exactly. It might not happen for a decade or more. But investors who do not know the full risks could be blown up. Addison Wiggin's *Little Book of the Shrinking Dollar* helps prepare the average American for anything that can happen. Read this book and be prepared."

—Bill Bonner, "The Daily Reckoning"

"People with income, savings, or investments denominated in the U.S. dollar—and that means all of us—face a period of great difficulty in the years ahead. To stay ahead of events, you'll want to keep this book close at hand."

—Charles Goyette, Bestselling Author of *Red and Blue and Broke All Over: Restoring America's Free Economy*

"This latest effort is a must read for investors and speculators whose wealth is denominated in U.S. dollars. While the topic is certainly not pleasant, this book is easy to read, and insightful."

—Rick Rule, Founder, Global Companies,
Sprott Asset Management

"*The Little Book of the Shrinking Dollar* will form part of one of the most important economic debates of our time."

—Tom Burroughes, Group Editor,
ClearView Financial Media, United Kingdom

"With *The Little Book of the Shrinking Dollar*, Addison has added to his legacy that began with *I.O.U.S.A.*, and has managed to extract new insights from the sordid tale of fiat currencies. He outlines where we are, how this can be corrected, and how to protect your purchasing power."

—Chuck Butler, President,
EverBank World Markets

"Addison Wiggin was among the first to highlight the extent of American indebtedness and to warn of its consequences, the most devastating of which will be the demise of the paper dollar. Addison's new book is a wake-up call to the private investor, full of astonishing statistics and thought-provoking investment ideas."

—Detlev Schlichter, Author,
Paper Money Collapse

"John Maynard Keynes: 'Lenin is said to have declared that the best way to destroy the Capitalist System was to debauch the currency . . . There is no subtler, no surer means of overturning the existing basis of society than to debauch the currency . . . and . . . in a manner which not one man in a million is able to diagnose.' Addison Wiggin is that 'one man in a million.'"

—Ralph Benko, Contributor, Forbes.com;
Principal, Capital City Partners, LLC

"The debasement of the U.S. dollar is a subject that Addison Wiggin has been commenting on with insight and forcefulness for a decade. His latest work is a valuable addition to our understanding of what is happening to the world's most important, and imperiled medium of exchange."

—Eric Sprott, Sprott Asset Management LP

THE LITTLE BOOK
OF
THE SHRINKING
DOLLAR

Little Book Big Profits Series

In the *Little Book Big Profits* series, the brightest icons in the financial world write on topics that range from tried-and-true investment strategies to tomorrow's new trends. Each book offers a unique perspective on investing, allowing the reader to pick and choose from the very best in investment advice today.

Books in the *Little Book Big Profits* series include:

THE LITTLE BOOK

OF

THE SHRINKING DOLLAR

What You Can Do to

Protect Your Money Now

ADDISON WIGGIN

WITH SAMANTHA BUKER

WILEY

John Wiley & Sons, Inc.

Published by John Wiley & Sons, Inc., Hoboken, New Jersey.
Published simultaneously in Canada.

For general information on our other products and services or for technical support, please contact our Customer Care Department within the United States at (800) 762-2974, outside the United States at (317) 572-3993 or fax (317) 572-4002.

Wiley also publishes its books in a variety of electronic formats. Some content that appears in print may not be available in electronic books. For more information about Wiley products, visit our web site at www.wiley.com..

Library of Congress Cataloging-in-Publication Data:

ISBN 978-1-118-24525-5 (cloth); 978-1-118-28317-2 (ebk);
978-1-118-28430-8 (ebk); 978-1-118-28506-0 (ebk)

Printed in the United States of America

10 9 8 7 6 5 4 3 2 1

For Jennifer, Meritt, Augie, and Lizzie

Contents

Acknowledgments

WHILE IT'S IMPOSSIBLE TO thank everyone who contributed to the ideas and arguments expressed in this book, the authors would like to thank the many people without whom the actual words selected would not have been possible.

Many thanks, of course, to the ever-patient Debra Englander, Kimberly Bernard, and Stacey Fischkelta at John Wiley & Sons.

We'd like to give a shout-out to our favorite experts in the financial and economic communities whose opinions we regard highly. Specifically, we'd like to thank those who've shared their ideas, forecasts, and advice with us for these pages: Chuck Butler, Peter Cooper, Michael Covel,

Charles Goyette, Byron King, John Mauldin, Christopher Mayer, the Honorable Dr. Ron Paul, Michael Pento, Rick Rule, Eric Sprott, Jeffrey Tucker, Tim Maurer, Marc Faber and Jim Rogers.

We owe a great debt to Ralph Benko, who applied his eyes to every page of this text and corrected us more than once, in tone and in fact. And a great many thanks go to our mentor, the incomparable Bill Bonner.

And finally, a special thanks to Samantha Buker. Sam is as astute a student as she is skilled as a writer. Without her diligence and hard work, this book would never have happened.

Introduction

What If the Power of Money Were in Your Hands?

————— ≈ —————

Sounding the Alarm about the U.S. Dollar

IF YOU PICKED UP this book, you realize the dollar isn't worth what it used to be. It's not just your Great Depression–era relatives saying it. If we go back just to the 1970s (when I was but a humble toddler), the dollar was worth a lot more.

What happened? Well, that's what this Little Book will tell you, with plenty of ways you can save the value of what you earn, and even profit, from the upheaval that dollar decline promises ahead.

Why am I so sure of the ultimate fate of the U.S. dollar? One simple fact: It's just paper.

Every paper currency in the history of civilization has eventually lost its entire value.

That's not to say that there won't be many stops along the way, pauses where the dollar rises against major currencies. However, today's situation is more urgent than ever because a paper currency that doesn't pay its holders a positive real interest rate tends to lose value at an accelerating rate. That describes the U.S. dollar (and most other currencies today).

The velocity of dollar-shrinkage has all the hallmarks of going into hyperdrive, but we won't know for sure the hour or the time. We don't know who will be in the White House when it happens, or who will be the Fed Reserve chair. But when the powers that be kick the final legs out from the stool propping up the dollar, the crash will be rapid.

That's why I'm writing this book, to prepare you for whatever lies ahead. There are moves you can put in place right now that can turn a profit in a week, some in six months, some in three years, and some are plain, good, long-term insurance that you can pass on to your children.

Here's How It Begins . . .

The whole basis for money itself—currency as a means of commerce—is based on tangible value. In other words, money is not the greenbacks we carry around. It is supposed to be the gold or other metal backing it up. The dollar is a promissory note. Check what it says at the top of the bill itself: "Federal Reserve Note."

Today, the American dollars in circulation are just a bunch of IOUs. That would be fine if the gold reserves were sitting in Fort Knox to back up those IOUs, but they are not. The Fed just keeps printing more and more money, and it will eventually catch up with us. The day will come when we will have to pay off those IOUs, not only domestically but to our ever-expanding foreign investors, too.

The Funny Money Game

History shows that money—official money printed by the government—has been known to lose value and become virtually worthless. Think back—50-million-mark bills from 1920s Germany, Russian rubles from pre-Revolution days, or Cuban pesos pre-Castro. In all these times and places, jarring political and economic changes destroyed currency values—suddenly, completely, and permanently.

We are not as insulated as many Americans believe. What kinds of events could do the same thing to the U.S.

dollar? What can you do today to position yourself strategically? There's plenty, which we'll explore in this book. In fact, the potential fall of the dollar can be good news—if you know what steps to take today.

Remember, a riverboat gambler who keeps asking for ever-higher markers will eventually run out of credit. At some point, the casino boss will realize that the gambler's ability to repay is questionable. Maybe those markers are just a heap of IOUs that can never be cashed in.

It All Began for Us in 1971

When the United States removed its currency from the gold standard, it seemed to make economic sense at the time. President Nixon saw this as the solution to a range of economic problems, and, combined with wage and price freezes, printing as much money as desired looked like a good idea. Unfortunately, most of the world's currencies followed suit. The world economy now runs primarily on a fiat money system, backed by nothing but air.

Fiat money is so-called because it is not backed by any tangible asset. That would be gold or silver. Heck, even seashells would be a better backing than the government's word for it. Instead, we must rely on the government's decree that "this money is a legal exchange medium, and it is worth what we say."

So, lacking a gold backing or backing of some other precious metal, what gives the currency value? Is there a special reserve somewhere? No. Some economists have tried to explain away the problems of fiat money by pointing to the vast wealth of the United States in terms of productivity, natural resources, and land. But even if those assets are counted, they're not liquid. They're not part of the system of exchange.

Here's a simple rule: Fiat money holds its value only as long as the people using that money continue to believe it has value—and as long as they continue to find people who will accept the currency in exchange for goods and services. The value of fiat money relies on confidence and expectation. So as we continue to increase our deficit bubbles and as long as consumer debt keeps rising, our fiat money will eventually lose value. Gold, in comparison, has tangible value based on real market forces of supply and demand.

The short-term effect of converting from the gold standard to fiat money has been widespread prosperity. So the overall impression is that U.S. monetary policy has created and sustained this prosperity. Why abandon the dollar when times are so good? Yet, things aren't as good right now.

This is where the great monetary trap is found. If we study the many economic bubbles in effect today, we know we eventually have to face up to the excesses, and that a big correction will occur. That means the dollar will fall and gold's value will rise as a direct result.

The sad lesson of economic history will be that when the gold standard is abandoned, and when governments can print too much money, they will. That tendency is a disaster for any economic system, because excess money in circulation (too much debt, in other words) only encourages consumer behavior mirroring that policy.

Thus, we find ourselves in record-high levels of credit card debt, refinanced mortgages, and personal bankruptcies—all connected to that supposed prosperity based on printing far too much currency: the fiat system.

"Whenever governments are granted the power to purchase their own debt, they never fail to do so, eventually destroying the value of the currency. Political money always fails because free people eventually reject it."

—*Dr. Ron Paul,* The Case for Gold

We can see where this overprinting will lead. Like a Tiananmen Square Rolex watch deal, the value simply isn't there.

In case you don't believe me, consider history.

Emperor Augustus started taking Rome down the slippery slope of decline back in 20 B.C. He started printing money faster than the gold could be produced to back it. He had the mines running 24 hours a day at the edges of the empire. Every emperor after followed suit. Nero wanted to continue the spending parade, mounting ever-larger trade deficits between Rome and its colonies and trading partners.

About 1,100 years ago, China began the paper money experiment. They called it "flying money" because a breeze could blow it out of a holder's hand. It was supposed to be a temporary fix during a copper shortage, but the paper money system got out of control. You see it was all too easy to just keep printing, which led to uncontrolled inflation. As bad an idea as it was, Marco Polo took some paper money back to Europe, where few people believed his tall tales of Chinese paper money, but a few hundred years later, the Europeans were ready to try their own paper money experiment.

When Spain found gold in Mexico in the sixteenth century, it became the world's richest nation. The Spanish used the gold to buy, buy, buy, and to expand their military influence. But the wars eventually used up their wealth, so Spain began issuing debt to pay the bills, leading to loss of its economic and military power. The French went through a similar period in the eighteenth century, printing way too much paper money and suffering unbelievable levels of inflation. That's thanks to excessive debt and a national bankruptcy.

I'm sure you're starting to sense a pattern. Runaway money printing leads to massive inflation and worthless currency. Perhaps the worst monetary collapse of the twentieth century was the so-called Weimar Republic. To handle post-World War I war reparations, the temporary government began printing massive amounts of currency to make payments. The currency became worthless. The resulting devastation paved the way for the Nazi movement and ushered in World War II.

The Last Time Money Was Worth Something

The year was 1944. For the first time in modern history, an international agreement was reached to govern monetary policy among nations. It was, significantly, a chance to create a stabilizing international currency and ensure monetary stability once and for all. In total, 730 delegates from 44 nations met for three weeks in July that year at a hotel resort in Bretton Woods, New Hampshire.

It was a significant opportunity, but it fell short of what could have been achieved. It was a turning point in monetary history, however.

The result of this international meeting, the Bretton Woods Accord, had the original purpose of rebuilding after World War II through a series of currency stabilization programs and infrastructure loans to war-ravaged nations. By 1946, the system was in full operation through the newly established International Bank for Reconstruction and Development (IBRD, the World Bank) and the International Monetary Fund (IMF).

What makes the Bretton Woods Accord so interesting to us today is the fact that the whole plan for international monetary policy was based on nations agreeing to adhere to a global *gold* standard. Each country signing the agreement promised to maintain its currency at values within a narrow margin to the value of gold. The IMF was established to facilitate payment imbalances on a temporary basis.

This system worked for 25 years. But it was flawed in its underlying assumptions. By pegging international currency to gold at $35 an ounce, it failed to take into consideration the change in gold's actual value since 1934, when the $35 level had been set. The dollar had lost substantial purchasing power during and after World War II, and as European economies built back up, the ever-growing drain on U.S. gold reserves doomed the Bretton Woods Accord's chances as a permanent, working system.

Now keep in mind that the United States owned 80 percent of the world's gold reserves at the time! So the

United States had every motive to agree to the use of the gold standard to organize world currencies and to create and encourage free trade. The gold standard evolved over a period of hundreds of years, planned by a central bank, government, or committee of business leaders.

The concept was a good one. However, in practice the international currency naturally became the U.S. dollar, and other nations pegged their currencies to the dollar rather than to the value of gold. The actual outcome of Bretton Woods was to replace the gold standard with the dollar standard. Once the United States linked the dollar to gold at a value of $35 per ounce, the whole system fell into place, at least for a while. Since the dollar was convertible to gold and other nations pegged their currencies to the dollar, it created a pseudo-gold standard.

But that's where the trouble starts.

How the Dollar Really Works

How do you define the worth of any commodity? Supply and demand. As demand increases, the price rises. That's efficiency.

But when paper money comes into use, the whole efficiency of the economic system goes out the window. That's because the government can print money (with a few keystrokes) out of thin air. So the money supply can continue to expand regardless of the real demand. It can do so even under a gold standard system, disregarding the supply of gold itself.

That's how paper money undoes itself and becomes worthless. We've seen it happen time and again, from ancient Rome, to China, to colonial Spain, to Germany, and now the United States.

Perhaps a paper money system pegged specifically to commodity reserves would give the currency the stability it needs and rein in government spending. The bottom line here is that the government is like a hungry fat man at an all-you-can-eat buffet—only with less discipline. They are simply going to print, print, print, until the system fails.

Never before in human history has the reserve currency of the world been so burdened with debt. (I write this knowing I said the same thing in 2008. It's only gotten worse.)

And never has the transfer of one international currency to another been peaceful. In 2008 we wondered, could the euro unseat the dollar? As we'll see further on, that's becoming increasingly unlikely—for the same reasons that the dollar can't hold its value.

There's just as much a chance that the new world reserve currency will be the Chinese yuan. But as we pointed out above, a government-controlled currency is as good as dead. It's just a matter of time.

Statist governments love to interfere and control the market. They found it necessary to eliminate the gold standard. They'll refuse to return to that kind of stability as long as they think they can get away with it.

So we soldier on under the price controls on the very symbol of our economic freedom—the U.S. dollar itself.

—Addison Wiggin
February 21, 2012

Chapter One

Dollar Decline

~

How Did We Get Here?

THINK THE DOLLAR HASN'T declined?

It has lost 80 percent of its purchasing power since 1970—the year before the great experiment of cutting the dollar loose from a fixed value in gold.

Back in 1970, if you just stashed a dollar coin under the mattress, today you'd find it buys you less than two dimes worth of goods. That doesn't even cover the price of a postage stamp or a can of Coke. It's practically worthless. (See Figure 1.1.)

Figure 1.1 The Dollar Deflated by the CPI

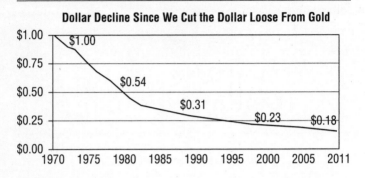

Source: See Testimony, Lewis E. Lehrman, March 17, 2011, before Congress.

Our currency is in a turbulent flux that's gotten worse and worse as the decades march on.

Today's dollar purchases five cents of what it purchased in the 1930s. Think that's too far back? Consider the 1980s. Today's dollar purchases only 50 cents of what it did back then.

But there will be critics who tell you that purchasing power isn't the only measure of currency strength.

Dollar's Popularity Doesn't Protect It

The U.S. Continental Congress created the U.S. dollar by an act of its own power in 1785. They hoped it would compete with the Spanish currency, which was the popular legal tender at the time.

Sure enough, here we are in 2012, and the U.S. dollar is now a victim of its own success. It's America's most successful export ever—more successful than Levi's, chewing gum, or Coca-Cola. No export is more popular. Let's look at the hard numbers.

Approximately two-thirds of U.S. dollars are held *outside* of the United States: 85 percent of global trade is made with the U.S. dollar. But all that stands to change.

I think the role of the U.S. dollar as the world's primary reserve currency will be gone in a decade. The foundation of our financial franchise, the US$ brand is trust. That's trust in our determination not to debase the world's primary exchange mechanism—the world's primary store of liquid wealth. We no longer deserve the trust, and are rapidly debasing the brand.

—Rick Rule, *Sprott Asset Management*

The euro is the second most popular currency in the world's beauty pageant, although it's taking a pretty ugly beating as we enter 2012. Still, about 26 percent of the world's monetary reserves holdings are denominated in this 17-nation currency.

We'll cover the details in later chapters, but for now, let's look at a few tremors we've tracked that predict an earthquake ahead for the U.S. dollar.

The Old Lady of Threadneedle Street to USA: You're Toast

Let me introduce you to my friend Ralph Benko, of the American Principles Project. We first met at the watershed October 2011 Heritage Foundation Conference on "The Stable Dollar: Why We Need It and How to Achieve It."

At the end of 2011, Ralph told *Forbes* readers, "The world dollar standard's death certificate arrives in the mail this week."

He's referring to a paper issued officially on December 20, 2011, by the Old Lady of Threadneedle Street—aka the Bank of England.

The Bank of England, as you can guess from the nickname is *the* staid, prosaic, conservative bunch on the block of central bankers.

So it's no surprise this working paper hides its revelation under the dull title, "Reform of the International Monetary and Financial System." But here's the dollar bomb: The world was better off when the world's currencies were tied to the dollar and the dollar was tied to gold—however tenuously.

To understand the dollar's future, it's important to understand the dollar's past.

By now, we have a vast cornucopia of dollar-denominated debt securities. The scale of these markets is unprecedented. The bigger the market the lower spreads it can offer, making deals here the most attractive.

There are also plenty of ways to hedge dollar exchange rate risk (which will be part of the solution set you'll learn about in this book). It's the reason why everyone from corporations to governments and central banks consider it a great currency for doing business. Finally, it's a safe haven that benefits from there being a lack of superliquid, high-volume alternatives. Australia, for instance, has recently made a reputation for stability, but it simply accounts for too small a slice of global financial transactions.

So, basically, the U.S. dollar just so happens to be winning the beauty contest among the ugliest world currencies.

Another friend, resource expert Rick Rule, agrees. "The only reason," he says, "we still enjoy the status that we enjoy globally—and the benefits of seigneurage—is that other societies have proven even better at debasement than we have. Basing your brand on the attribute of being the least bad has been a consistently faulty strategy."

How do you know when your branding campaign isn't working? When consumers start buying from your competitors in increasing numbers. The same principle is at work with currencies.

Increasingly, we'll have to compete for our dollars to be used, bought, and saved.

Here's an early sign.

Russia and Iran Are Ditching the Dollar

The two countries will carry out their trade with each other using rubles and rials. Add that to the list. China and Russia abandoned the greenback in their bilateral trade more than a year ago.

The big rumble is that the Middle East will follow suit. Imagine if they no longer trade oil in U.S. dollars. It won't just be Iran as some "alternative" bourse. Plans are at work for a Gulf States cooperation, including Saudi Arabia and Abu Dhabi.

This shouldn't be too surprising, given that the United Nations itself has called for a "new global reserve currency." Why? They say it's dangerous to allow us the "privilege" of building up our massive trade deficit.

"Pretty soon," says EverBank's currency guru Chuck Butler, "having the reserve currency of the world isn't going to be such a big thing, if all the commodity trade isn't settled in dollars!"

Chuck is definitely in the camp that questions the safe haven currency status the dollar holds.

He doesn't blame any country for wanting to remove dollars from their reserves. After all, the dollars have lost so much value over the years.

Sure, he points out, it is the most liquid currency in the world, but if countries keep taking dollars out of the terms of their trade, how much longer can it remain the most liquid currency?

It's a real conundrum that any dollar earner (and investor) needs to be aware of. It doesn't mean we'll lose the world's preferred currency status today, tomorrow, or even next year.

Eventually, though, there will come a time when the world's nations will stop adding U.S. dollars to their already swollen coffers. They'll demand something else instead.

We would argue, like the Old Lady of Threadneedle Street, for something that looks a lot more like Bretton Woods.

We're betting other nations (especially the gold-hoarding ones we'll explore in later chapters) would totally agree.

Let us put a period on this by ending with the comment from England's central bank researchers. The Bretton Woods era "stands out as coinciding with remarkable financial stability and sustained high growth at a global level."

Sounds pretty nice, doesn't it?

They go on: "the solid growth outcomes were not simply the result of post-war reconstruction efforts." They say that in fact, GDP growth was actually stronger in the 1960s than it was in the 1950s.

Makes you wonder: What went wrong?

Chapter Two

Serial Bubble Blowers

~

Who Controls Our
Economic Destiny?

THE SHRINKING DOLLAR IS a modern problem. The U.S. dollar has been shrinking since the inception of the Federal Reserve—the very crew assigned the task of maintaining its value. Of late, the decline is accelerating at an alarming rate.

For many Americans, the suggestion that the dollar is losing value is unthinkable—even unpatriotic. The problem is not simply a lack of understanding about the nature of wealth and investment used to sustain it. Our policy makers and economists make no distinction between wealth created through savings and investment in the real economy versus "wealth" created in the markets through asset bubbles brought about by credit policies.

When I tell people this, I feel like I'm addressing a meeting of folks who want to lose weight at the local burger joint. We as individuals—and as a nation—are addicted to cheap, easy credit. What the government gives, we'll take. We spend at a high level, and we want to accumulate wealth on the same fast track.

Forget hard work, we'd rather our house go up in value like magic! Traditionally, economists recognized that it took time to build an estate. People and countries could build wealth slowly. Those days are far, far behind us. Now we are at the mercy of what I call serial bubble blowers.

All the U.S. economy's so-called improvements stem from one main reason: all economic growth during the "recovery" since 2001 can be traced to a seemingly endless array of asset and borrowing bubbles.

First, we saw the stock market bubble, then the bond bubble, then the housing bubble, then the mortgage refinance bubble, then the commodities bubble. Now another bond bubble approaches.

In between, we haven't seen a single sign of stable, sustained growth. And that makes sense; consumer spending has been surging in excess of disposable income for years. That's not real growth.

Right now, Washington thinks that another round of stimulus will solve the problem. That's like saying that overeating will eventually lead to serious dieting. Consumer spending isn't juicing the economy.

Meanwhile, since the government is broke, all the borrowing they do to fund stimulus, tax cuts, and anything else to save the economy puts us at the mercy of foreign investors. If and when they decide to slash their investments in U.S. dollars or Treasury securities, we'll have a crash landing worse than anything we've seen yet.

It'll be far worse than Lehman Brothers' collapse, far worse than 2008's aftermath.

We depend on foreign investors for everything. Be they private, institutional, or governmental, we need them. If the dollar's fall frightens foreign owners, they will sell from this immense stock of dollar assets.

But how big are these foreign holdings? You rarely hear about this on financial news channels, so you probably don't think it's a big deal. In fact, it's a big fat deal.

We're sitting on $15.4 trillion in debt. How is it going to get paid? And by whom?

Back before 1970, foreigners held a 5 percent slice of U.S. public debt. Today foreigners hold nearly half the pie. And the government owes a bunch of it to itself—$4.6 trillion—including what it's borrowed from the Social Security trust fund.

Is Washington at all alarmed? While the end of 2011 did culminate in near-monthly government shutdown threats, we expect the debt ceiling to go on being raised as it was under every presidency since, well, 1917, when we had a World War to finance.

At last count, it's been raised 74 times. And lest you believe the crisis came to a head in the Obama administration, we'd like to point out that he's only raised it three times so far. Famed fiscal conservative Ronald Reagan raised it a whopping 18 times. So you see borrowing to spend is everyone's favorite game. Darn all the consequences.

Why Isn't All This Intervention Working?

As usual, the hope is that a cheaper dollar makes exports cheaper and reduces our trade deficit. A nice thought, of course, but past experience shows that this is unlikely.

What's the real cause of the trade deficit? Chronically high levels of undersaving and underinvestment.

The catch is that everything the Fed is doing right now only encourages two things: undersaving and underinvestment.

When you monkey with interest rates, the way the Fed is wont to do, you're able to send false signals to potential investors and savers.

In essence, the Fed is telling you that you don't know what to do with your own money. To them, you're an individual who's too stupid to know what's best. They don't think you can safely and simply buy the goods and services you need—or want—when and as you need or want them.

To get out of the dot-com hangover, the Fed redirected our attention to housing. By offering us ever-lower interest rates, they encouraged mortgage borrowing on an unprecedented scale. On cue, they allowed two near-bankrupt public agencies—Fannie Mae and Freddie Mac—to huddle under government's protective wing. These guys are worse than pawnshop brokers, yet they pretend to enable the American dream.

And besides, why would you put aside money to *save* for a house, when your next-door neighbor is offered a no-money down loan with an adjustable rate in a much better neighborhood than you ever dreamed you could afford?

Banks get way more money off that kind of deal, as long as the party lasts and the money is flowing, than they ever would taking your nice little deposits and lending them out. Likewise, they're not rewarding you for saving to consume later.

Right now, we've almost gotten to the point where you'll be paying the bank to keep your money safe. Forget an interest-bearing account when rates are so low . . . and inflation kicks into high gear.

The same goes for business, when faced with "free" money, allocations go way out of whack. Debt-fueled takeovers become the backbone of the market. Forget stockholders buying into a good business that's developing inventive new products that change the world for the better. The herd would rather bet on derivatives on mortgages—until that bubble burst.

Then, like heaping 10-ton barrels of kerosene on a house fire, bailouts have become the norm. So in that case, we're stuck in a nightmare of garbage-in, garbage-out. Banks keep getting bigger by getting government assistance to help buy out their weaker brothers. It should come as no surprise when Bank of America slips under $5, but the powers that be don't like that.

The huge credit and debt bubbles are a sign of a dislocated and imbalanced economy. We're sitting on excess capacity in most areas of the economy (like finance and construction) and insufficient capacity in others (like agriculture and energy). This goes beyond the United States to the entire global economy.

When we still see near $100 oil and high food prices—despite near 9 percent unemployment—we're seeing evidence of sectors starved of needed investment.

Bubblicious

If you look at the Fed's track record, you'll see that the only thing they are capable of doing is pushing up the price of stocks!

How's that work? Well, first off, their near-zero interest rate policy means you get paid a measly 0.25 percent chunk of interest by the bank. So you'd be a fool to keep your money there!

So you look toward something more adventuresome, but safe. Corporate bonds? Well, that's a great idea, but nowadays companies like Procter & Gamble or PepsiCo can sell large bundles of notes for next to nothing.

So-called safe sovereign debt yields squat. You'd have to turn to something high risk. Try Greece. Ha.

And then you have to consider inflation. If our Fed wise men consider 2 percent per year inflation rates ideal, then you've gotta at least find an investment that pays you 2 percent or more.

That means for the safe crowd, dividend-paying stocks will take off. For those who actually want a return on their money, they've got to go all-in on stocks.

But wait, you say, didn't this whole thing start off with a stock bubble? Well, you're right.

Albert Einstein's famous definition of insanity is "doing the same thing over and over again and expecting different results." As you'll see over and over again in the pages of this book, that's exactly what central bankers are doing around the globe.

When our false optimism is not rewarded, the experts will no longer be able to argue away the dollar's weakness.

Under a truly free system of currency markets, the dollar would have collapsed long ago. However, in an effort to keep its currency cheap against the dollar, China has almost single-handedly prevented this. Their persistence traps other Asian countries to do the same.

Initially, our friends over at the fledgling European Central Bank said they were opposed to such credit interventions. They viewed artificial tinkering in currency markets as a way to fuel credit excess. This view was right, of course. But now that they're in trouble, they'll welcome any tinkering anyone cares to lend, including and most especially the United States.

The only real solution would be to let competitive forces replace currency intervention as international policy.

How Does Money Printing Work?

Explaining how the Fed's money printing destroys the dollar's value is pretty easy. Consider a more physical, real example.

Back in the late 1800s, the island of Yap, tucked away in the Pacific Ocean, didn't use dollars or pounds sterling, or gold of any kind. They used stones for money. Called rai, these limestone rocks don't strike us as the simplest currency. The largest stones weighed many tons. Weight = value. Pretty simple, right?

Why were these stones worth so much? Not only were they heavy, they were brought from an island over 155 miles away. This perilous journey over rough seas wasn't easy. Many stones were lost at sea, along with the men who carted them hence.

So the risk in procuring the money stones was the thing that gave it value. Added value came if many men died to get it, or conversely, if none died at all.

As you can imagine, the supply was very limited. And since they were so heavy, the Yapese had a hard time ripping off each other's net worth.

All that fell apart in 1874. All it took was one savvy, shipwrecked Irish-American named David O'Keefe. He helped the Yapese to import whole shiploads of large stones far more easily than they could do in the past. He oversaw the importing of money, which he then traded for actual goods like sea cucumbers and copra.

So the Yapese were bringing thousands of stones to their island, debasing the value of their families' inherited wealth.

Today, you can traipse around the island and still see these amazing four-ton stones. But they're basically worthless.

The Fed is doing the same thing to your family's wealth!

It can increase the money supply anytime it wants. The money it creates comes as if out of thin air.

Now let's think about it with the Yap example. The more stones, the less value. The situation is the same here. The more dollars we have floating around for transactions, the less value each dollar is going to have. Yes, it's just that simple.

Likewise, the price of everything will go up. If everyone has more dollars to chase a limited supply of goods they wish to purchase, the possessor of goods can charge whatever he wants.

That's why when currency troubles start to grow the first thing the government tries to do is make it illegal for businesses to raise prices.

But there's nothing that shackles the Fed; no external impediment keeps it from producing as many dollars as it pleases.

Ideally, it uses masses of equations about spending, inflation, and a host of other measures to decide the exact right amount of money in the market and keep to it. But this they rarely if ever do.

Eventually, we'll be like the Yapese. We'll look on the U.S. dollar as an amusing yet worthless kind of trinket.

When the Magic of Money Printing Wears Off

Central banks no longer print money. . . . Money is "created" by tapping out a few strokes on a computer keyboard. . . . Don't you wish you could put money in your bank account, by just entering the amount you wish to add, via your keyboard, into your computer?

Of course you do. So why is what is desirable yet highly illegal for us, good enough for our government?

We've struck a devil's bargain. Central bankers hold all the power over our money. They determine the supply and damage its worth. And they are but puppets of the government. We quit the gold standard, removing the only objective way to determine the value of cash.

Why did we take the devil's hand? Because we were told that central banks would *increase* stability in markets. That vigilance on the part of these smart men would keep the value of our dollar steady. Heh.

Let's just look at the number of crises.

While we were on a version of the gold standard known as the Bretton Woods Exchange Rate System, we had one crisis every decade, on average. That seems like a lot, yes?

After 1971, when we cut our last ties to gold and put all faith in the great central banks, did we do better? No. We now enjoy about two crises *per year*!

Does that seem like stability to you?

Running Out of Tricks

Right now, the Fed chairman has very few tools at his disposal.

Under his call, in 2008, the central bank cut its main conventional tool for slowing down and speeding up economic growth—the Fed funds interest rate—to near zero. But that didn't pull us out of recession.

Next, he tried the unconventional.

He exploded the Fed's balance sheet by buying up $2.3 trillion worth of bonds to drive down borrowing costs even further. (For this you can bet he was criticized for risking a weaker dollar and inviting inflation to come knocking!)

Now the Fed Chair is focused on replacing maturing securities with longer-dated bonds . . . but that's still not enough juice.

His job, though you might not guess it, is to ensure maximum employment and stable prices. Yes, sometimes we do pity him, but that's what Congress insists he do according to the Federal Reserve Act.

Here's just how desperate the Fed is to influence markets.

Starting in 2012, the once super-secret Jackson Hole crew will now begin publishing its policy makers' forecasts for interest rates—most importantly signaling when interest rates will rise.

Naturally, the move is billed as a new approach to deliver greater clarity about what the Fed is up to. Really, it seems like a last-ditch effort to tip their hand and control what the stock market is doing—via the media.

What kind of card game is this? After each meeting they'll publish the projected appropriate level for the main Fed funds rate in the final quarter of the current year, plus the next few years.

These projections are like a wink to the market, saying, "Here's what we're gonna do." With the mere hint, investors will start acting as though the moves have already happened.

For instance, over in the bond market, instead of having to directly intervene, they'll only have to tell bond investors what they expect the main target fund rate to be. As of now, bond market investors only make guesses in the direction they'll be headed. With speech alone, the Fed will be able to flatten the yield curve as investors expect bond yields to flatten across the spectrum of Treasuries from short-to-long.

The Fed has already pledged to stay near zero out to 2014. Will it be longer? Until we have these projections coming, it's anyone's guess. When the rates do go up, the Fed doesn't want there to be any surprises.

Like a good confidence game, this trick will work, so long as everyone keeps believing in it. Unfortunately, as the old-timers say, in any con game, if you don't know who the mark is—you're the mark!

Who Chooses These Guys?

These guys aren't actually superheroes, but they do wield some pretty amazing powers—like creating money. The eight meetings they hold per year determine our monetary policy. Here in the United States, the president nominates all seven governors on the Federal Reserve's board. That board, in turn, is the majority of the 12-member voting powers on the Federal Open Market Committee.

Congress has the final say of approval on the president's nominees.

While you might say this scenario offers some checks and balances . . . notice also that all the people who hold the power in this situation may not be lifetime policy wonks. Instead, they're something almost worse: they're constantly running for the next election. And nothing is better for elections than kick-payments-down-the-road stimulus enabled by loose monetary policy!

What Occupy Wall Street Got Right

A recent *Huffington Post* article by Alexander Eichler proclaimed the following:

> The financial industry may have taken a hit during the Great Recession . . . but the financial sector represents a bigger share of the economy today than it did in 2006, recent Commerce Department figures show—despite the bailouts, bank failures and political efforts at reform that have taken place since.

Despite the bailouts, bank failures and political efforts? He could have said "because of" and be telling the truth.

The financial sector counts for 8.9 percent of our GDP. It generates 29 percent of all the profits in America. At its 2001 peak, that figure accounted for 46 percent—that's almost half of America's business! No wonder it got too big to fail.

On the flipside, consider that the financial sector is the second-largest group doling out donations to Congress and presidents. Unlike the biggest group—unions—which contribute mostly to Democrats, financial lobbyists spread the dough evenly between the two parties. That's the way to get taken care of when times are tough, and keep the profits when the money is rolling!

Here's the trick . . . no one in charge wants sound money—most definitely not the big banks!

Think of it like this. The foreign exchange market got its start in the 1970s, and business has been booming ever since! The turnover in these markets is in excess of $4 trillion per day. That includes all sorts of transactions:

- Spot transactions
- Forward contracts
- Foreign exchange swaps
- Currency swaps
- Options and other products

Who'd want to lose all that great action? Certainly not the top 10 traders in currency: Deutsche Bank, Barclays, UBS, Citi, J.P. Morgan, HSBC, Royal Bank of Scotland, Credit Suisse, Goldman Sachs, Morgan Stanley.

Well sometimes the "can't beat 'em, join 'em" motto is worth following. One new solution to get small cumulative gains (with the occasional home run) in the currency market is actually really easy to do.

SOLUTION!

Binary Options to the Rescue

Currency trading has a well-deserved reputation for being confusing and risky. So most investors stay away—not even trying to collect the gigantic profits forex traders could see.

But recent innovations make currency trading easier, safer, and potentially more profitable than ever before. With simple bets on the U.S. dollar's rise or fall, you can rack up gains of 124 percent in 15 days . . . 61 percent in 4 days . . . and 136 percent in 9 days.

To participate, you don't have to be chained to your computer to get in and out of these trades. You don't need to learn jargon like "pip" or "lot size." And you don't have to keep track of delivery months or contract specifications. Thanks to this latest market innovation, all those worries are obsolete.

They're called binary options. Until just a few short years ago, they were only available in the United States to professional and institutional investors.

Binaries trade on the North American Derivatives Exchange, or Nadex (www.nadex.com), covering a wide list of strategies and investments. Binaries are tradable contacts that let you bet on whether something will happen or not. I call them "yes" or "no" bets.

In a way, they resemble sports bets—like betting the Colts will win on Sunday or that Alex Rodriguez will hit more than 30 home runs in a season. But binaries standardize and focus on financial markets and economic events. You can bet whether gold will go above a certain price or a currency will fall to a certain level.

(*Continued*)

What Occupy Wall Street Is Missing

My colleague, Jeffrey Tucker over at Laissez Faire Books, recently reminded me of this simple quote: "You can obey balance sheets or bullies."

What he means is that we can have one of two things. We can have a price system, or we get top-down folks who try to control everything. The two approaches don't combine well, as we've been finding out over the last few decades.

We prefer the bottoms-up method. Price signals come from voluntary exchanges between individuals and businesses, between businesses and banks, between banks and individuals. That's the best system: the free market *laissez-faire* price system. It works best without constant false signals or outright market manipulations.

Price is simple. Say you want to buy a loaf of bread. You as consumer would like to pay as little as possible for it. Heck, you'd like a free loaf of bread like the manna in the Bible. The baker, however, would like to charge more. Yet, he'll settle for as much as bread buyers seem willing to pay. The price you pay is the result of this agreement.

This exchange is practically as old as barter. It's arrived at without speaking a word, yet it reflects the sum total of many pieces of information: the availability of flour, salt, water, human taste and preference, alternative products being offered, and so on.

And it all happens without a central planner. No central board of experts tells us what the prices should be.

You don't need to rely on genius in this system, and that's a blessing. The system is so simple, it *is* genius. Finding good central bankers is so hard, we'd be better off not having to find them in the first place.

No institution can compete with this efficiency, however much it may try. The same goes for our money supply.

If the money supply weren't constantly in flux and growing, the value of the dollar would be a simple number that never lies. The balance sheet, likewise, tells you clearly what's sustainable and what's not.

Today's balance sheets—monitored by everyone from the SEC to the Treasury—don't really follow the rules. They don't even mark most assets to the market price!

Without interventions and bailouts, if you spend more than you make, you will go belly up. If you take in more money than you spend, you grow. This simple arithmetic rule can decide who's profitable and who's not. It determines how resources should be used.

In a world like ours, where bullies reign over our money, it's only a matter of time before they falter. There will be more black swan surprises like Lehman Bros. And mistakes compound. The consequences of asset bubbles are unpredictable. Unless the government manages every single aspect of the market, true prices will eventually be discovered. So crashes will continue to be erratic and unpredictable, their destruction swift.

No one human—much less a central board—can foresee every possible use for our capital and resources, and manage the economy accordingly.

The market economy is not some superior organism greater than the sum of its parts. The economy doesn't have its own goals. It does not exist to generate positive GDP. It does not give guaranteed employment.

The economy only exists because you do. It exists for your needs and wants alone. What makes it tick best is consent, not force. The participants have to make smart decisions. They have to be ready to accept the consequences.

It's a pretty big responsibility, the onus is on you!

So while you're right to be concerned about Social Security or Medicare (since you already paid into the swindle), the bigger danger is your nest egg that's in your hands today. Comfortable savings by today's standards could become worthless when you retire.

With that in mind, let's turn to the next chapter and see where Americans went wrong and what we can do to change things now.

Economic Reality Check

*America's Consumption
Can't Save It*

SORRY TO SAY THIS, but we have to face it: There's no such thing as bringing the economy back to where it was.

We don't mean to be Negative Nellies, but the years before the recession were fundamentally weak. Before the recession, according to Columbia University researcher Bruce Greenwald, the bottom 80 percent of Americans had been spending around 110 percent of their income.

As we concluded in the last chapter, without the help of mass delusion and collusion, such spending is simply not sustainable.

The collusion and delusion we enjoyed for a spell came from thinking that our homes were our great collateral—ever-expanding in value. We thought we could borrow against it until we died and that our children could maybe still turn a profit on the house.

Alan Greenspan and Ben Bernanke, as chairmen of the Fed, were head engineers in this great bubble experiment. Through low interest rates and nonregulation—not even using what regulatory tools they had, they enabled the banks to lend, lend, lend.

We know how it turned out. But what's it look like ahead?

We're at record low fixed mortgage rates: 3.91 percent. The rate has only dipped this low one other time in history! That spells unprecedented opportunity for the few that can afford to borrow or are in the bank's good graces enough to refinance.

But we see little effect. We clocked out 2011 with the most dismal new home sales record in half a century. Old homes are selling at a rate barely better than in the 2010 slump.

Mortgage rates usually track Treasuries, whose yield is also plummeting. If the Fed does another round of bond purchasing, expect this rate to get even lower.

How long should it take? A year? A decade?

What makes a real housing market thrive? Higher employment and higher wages. Neither of which is growing right now. At least not naturally. Sure, there were temporary jobs like the 2011 Census.

Speaking of the census, most of the news wasn't good. We're not adding consumers. In fact, we're losing them, and fast: 48 percent of America qualifies as "low income." (No wonder we aren't collecting much in taxes.) There are more Americans living under extreme poverty than have ever been recorded.

Since 2009, we've added another 4 million souls to the category low-income-to-below-the-poverty line. That's 146.4 million people in America who aren't consuming much aside from ever-increasing applications for food stamps. One out of every seven Americans depends on this aid.

Do they sound like potential homebuyers to you?

If you're unlucky enough to get laid off or fired, your average time on unemployment is up to 40 weeks. Between 2004 and 2007, the average out-of-work period was more like two months! And now, the longer you're on the unemployment roster, the less likely you are to get rehired in today's environment.

The most toxic zones are Florida, New Jersey, Illinois, or Nevada. Over 50 percent of the unemployed have been so for over six months! It shouldn't surprise you that these are some of the same places where housing prices soared and collapsed first and hardest. Or, in the case of New Jersey, recall that famous slogan splayed across a (now-rusting) Delaware River bridge-span: "Trenton Makes—The World Takes." That slogan dates back to 1910. That was before the Federal Reserve . . . that was back when the dollar was worth the same as it was in 1792.

But here's the economist's Catch-22 . . . were we to resurrect manufacturing, they now say, we'll have to have as cheap a dollar as we can get away with to remain competitive. (Although we'd like to point out this is not the case with the euro's stronghold, Germany.)

But back to canvassing for available U.S. consumers. . . .

One in five people lucky enough to hold a job consider themselves underemployed. That's made up of folks who are employed part time, but would rather have full-time work. In 2010 and 2011, that number topped 20 percent. It hovers above 18 percent as I type.

Do you think they'll power back the economy?

According to the Brookings Institution, who has exhaustively modeled job losses since 2008, we're looking at a tough climb.

If the economy adds 208,000 jobs per month—the average monthly rate for the best year of job creation in the past decade—it'll take us until March 2024 to return to prerecession levels of employment.

If you're an optimist, and predict a job creation rate like in the 1990s, we'll close the jobs gap by February 2017.

Based on December 2011's addition of 200,000 jobs, I'd say it'll likely take more than a decade.

Solution!

Look for Companies Supplying Basic, Need-Based Products; Ideally Ones That Pay a Nice Dividend

Think Clorox (NYSE:CLX) and Procter & Gamble (NYSE:PG).

Pick a Few Companies That Cater to the 1 Percent

Their slice of the pie keeps growing. Real luxury goods like Patek Phillipe watches and Bugatti cars hold value and outpace inflation.

Consider this: Back in 2008, when the world was falling apart, an analyst I know wouldn't touch Tiffany's stock with a barge pole! He advised readers to stick to essentials, not "trinkets."

What happened? Tiffany & Co. stock shot up from a low under $20 per share to more than $80!

And it's not the first time this stock did well in tough times. All-time great investor Peter Cundill wrote about picking up shares in the 1970s for under $10. Then the company recorded its first $1 million profit. He more than doubled his money.

(Continued)

Are You a Little More Adventurous?

Add stocks in developing and emerging markets that cater specifically to their growing middle class.

You can focus on the BRIC nations (Brazil, Russia, India, China), but also consider countries like Colombia, Vietnam, Singapore, or even Mongolia. The second-largest population of high net worth individuals (HNWIs) resides in the Asia-Pacific region. And sales of luxury goods here are definitely up!

Why Colombia? Well, it's already put its housing bubble behind it, and its middle class now makes up over a quarter of its population, over 13 million strong.

What We Need Is More Manufacturing

In 1950, manufacturing jobs employed one-third of America's workforce. Today we're down to one-tenth of Americans holding manufacturing jobs. The pace of that decline sped up in the last decade or so.

There are two reasons: (1) increases in productivity and (2) globalization.

The majority of jobs lost in the last decade come from productivity, not outsourcing. This is the same kind of revolution that took Americans out of agriculture and looking for work elsewhere.

Today's flight is from goods production to service sector jobs . . . but so far the growth hasn't benefited the

average American by as much, at least not when it
comes to wages. (The only real benefit you see is the fact
that a flat screen TV is so cheap—thanks to exported
parts from Asia—you can sit on your couch and feel like
king!)

Let's consider what goes into an iPhone. A look at
its guts come from shows you how we've racked up
the deficit with the whole of Asia.

iPhone's screen comes from Japan. Taiwan
the battery chargers, camera lenses, and timing
plus a bunch of chips from Taiwan Semiconductor
Manufacturing Company. The video processing chip
comes from South Korea. In all, nine countries produce
the parts that are sent to China for assembly.

But wait, isn't tech the category where we are still the
leader? Labor in Japan or Taiwan isn't cheap—not by a
long shot.

Forget the old encouragement to buy American. It's
simply not possible any longer because so many of the
products we purchase are being manufactured in China,
India, and other Asian and Central American countries.
So we can't buy American any longer. Today, your only
choice is to spend American.

This tectonic shift in how the U.S. economy works
can be described as the replacement of real capitalism
with a kind of show-business fictitious capitalism. The

overall effect of the lauded information age didn't create a new economic miracle.

Consider the example that Peter Thiel, one of the world's most successful technology investors gives. Twitter. It may have a lot of users, but it doesn't do much to employ Americans. "Five hundred people will have job security for the next decade," Thiel told the *New Yorker*, "but how much value does it create for the entire economy?" As he puts it, "We wanted flying cars, instead we got 140 characters."

From 2002 to 2007, spending on IT and hardware made up around 2 percent of the GDP pie. Now it makes up less than 1 percent. If you throw in the communications industry, you'll bring the GDP contribution to 4.6 percent. Wow, that's hardly a bastion of growth. The biggest contributor by far is the federal government. Finance, of course, is a good 20 percent contributor.

Meanwhile, gains we saw in construction, commercial banking, and real estate were all directly tied to the burst housing and mortgage refinancing bubbles.

European economists realize that productivity growth isn't the be-all and end-all. It's actually part of a more important trend: capital investment.

American economists don't like to go there, because it brings up the real problem with the relationship between employment and the value of the dollar.

As a rule, where there is high capital investment, high productivity growth can be taken for granted. Capital investment, by the way, also provides the increase in demand and spending necessary to translate growing productivity into effectively higher employment and true economic growth.

History is our testament: Creation of jobs is part of the creation of infrastructure. The building of the great railroads and canals in the 1800s created unprecedented economic growth and jobs. The 1930s dam and public works projects were but a pale echo of those great achievements.

American economists, however, cling to the hope that high productivity growth goes hand in hand with jobless economic growth. It's possible, sure, but it's worth pointing out that this hasn't happened before.

In the United States, net capital investment has collapsed. As resource investor Rick Rule puts it: "We, as a society have lived beyond our means for at least two decades. We consume more than we produce, and hence 'cannibalize' our capital." Anyone who believes monetary policy alone will breathe life into our economy will be disappointed. That idea is a distraction, and a dangerous one.

The theory to our nation's present monetary course is that low inflation allows money printing. The increased money supply allows for ever-growing levels of consumer debt. Consumer debt leads to more consumer spending, and more spending is considered equal to prosperity.

Et voilà, that's how you spend your way back to a healthy economy.

Does that sound like a great economic plan to you? Think about it. A shot of whiskey makes you feel good, right? But do 20 shots in a single evening, and it could darn well kill you.

Same goes for monetary policy. Those on high should be smart and brave enough to ask: How much credit growth can we really afford?

The conservative (and we happen to think) correct answer is not so generous. This theory would limit credit growth so that we never exceed savings.

If we revisit the housing bubble for a minute . . . we'd realize that this conservative theory exactly explains the problem with what the Feds did in tandem with the mortgage lenders.

What actually happened was no-holds-barred lending for zero-down, extended to anyone via robo-signing. We bet even the family dog could have gotten an ARM mortgage in 2005.

If instead, the supply and demand for lendable funds (i.e., savings) had determined mortgages, the housing bubble would never have been big enough to matter.

The longer we continue the inflating cycle of asset bubbles, the longer it'll take for the economy to find its true footing. In other words, if we're to know where we're at fiscally, we should never allow our liabilities to exceed our assets.

Today, the Fed keeps interest rates artificially low to juice spending. This rate is completely doctored. It does not depend on purchasing coming from savings. Nor does it consider limitations on the circulation of currency.

However, it's no good to say "the government made me do it." That's not helping the millions walking away from foreclosed homes nor the 36 million Americans sitting on outstanding Fed-guaranteed loans.

Yes, the Fed did backstop lenders Fannie Mae and Freddie Mac by flushing $169 billion into their coffers since 2008. The hope is that they'll save these borrowers . . . but really the idea is to clear out the inventory of unsold homes even faster. How? You got it, by juicing the system with another round of credit easing and lower mortgage rates.

Our whole financial system is pretty much like the factory run by the Once-ler in Dr. Seuss's immortal book *The Lorax*. It's biggering and biggering—hawking stuff from shoddy mortgages to complex financial products—like the "Thneed"—which nobody wants but everyone needs.

We could easily see the role of the Once-ler played by a former Fed chair. But we could only wish a *Financial Times* op ed might read like more like this: "I meant no harm. I most truly did not. But I had to grow bigger. So bigger

I got. I went right on biggering . . . selling more Thneeds. And I biggered my money, which everyone needs."

Instead, as we entered 2012, Alan Greenspan wrote:

> The welfare state has run up against a brick wall of economic reality and fiscal book-keeping. Congress, having enacted increases in entitlements without visible means of funding them, is on the brink of a stalemate. . . .
>
> We face a true revolution, not so much in the streets but in the fundamental choices the American people will have to make to secure our fiscal future. Arithmetic demands it.

That's the catch. This money-creation spending spree machine produces big byproducts . . . worse than "Gluppity Glup" and "Shloppity Shlop." Try inflation! Try more job losses! Try banking crises!

And to think we criticize China for having complete government control over their currency and their banking system. We're in the same exact boat; it just doesn't appear that way.

Do you ever notice how in the press releases it's always "we're doing this because we need to get the 'American consumer back on his feet'"?

Of course, everyone who's ever had a seven-year-old knows how this story ends: "Now all that was left 'neath the bad-smelling sky was my big empty factory . . . the

Lorax . . . and I." (The Lorax, of course, has the sense to hitch himself up and disappear through the last clean patch between the clouds.)

Solution!

Look for Blue Chip Stocks That Rake Most of Their Revenue from Overseas

Nearly one out of every five S&P 500 companies now generates a majority of its sales overseas. (Coca-Cola is perhaps the iconic example: 74 percent of its revenue comes from outside the States.)

Those stand to be among the best performers among the blue chips in the years ahead. They're exposed to healthier business environments overseas. And they'll be insulated from the shock of a weakening dollar. Consider Table 3.1 as a starting place.

Table 3.1   Looking Overseas: The Top 10 U.S. Companies Ranked by Overseas Revenue

Company	Percent of Overseas Revenues
Philip Morris Intl. Inc.	100.00
Newmont Mining Corp.	95.19
Nividia Corp.	91.70
Advanced Micro Devices Inc.	87.38
Texas Instruments Inc.	87.29
Qualcomm Inc.	86.87
Intel Corp.	84.30
Applied Materials Inc.	84.03
Aes Corp.	80.60
Colgate Palmolive Co.	80.27

Source: Addison Wiggin's Apogee Advisory.

While you can't just up and leave that easily, there's plenty you can do to get your money elsewhere—to greener pastures. Consider following the lead of the biggest blue chips or go beyond BRICs.

SOLUTION!

Go Beyond BRICs—Once-in-a-Lifetime Opportunities in Frontier Markets

"Frontier investors," says Leopard Capital's Doug Clayton, "seek to make outsized returns by investing in countries before they become popular. They are our modern-day pioneers, seeking out places that mainstream investors are hardly aware of, that are quietly in transition toward becoming tomorrow's emerging markets."

Is every frontier market a good place to invest? Hardly. "But the better ones are unbeatable," Doug told us over dinner in Medellín, Colombia. "They are either 'least-developed countries' finally getting their act together or post-conflict countries at last on the mend. These can offer once-in-a-lifetime opportunities for resolute investors."

How can you tell a frontier market from an emerging market? "If it is easy to raise money for them, or they have an ETF or are heralded on a mainstream magazine cover," Doug says, "they are no longer a frontier market." That's why he says Colombia is "too far along" for his taste.

Here's how to tell a frontier market's calling card: "What the most interesting frontier markets have in common," says Doug, "are rapid growth rates, unleveraged economies, cheap expanding forces due to youthful demographics and underutilized natural resources. Usually, their physical infrastructure is getting better every year, not deteriorating like in the West."

Some intriguing options we've found: Cambodia, Rwanda, Haiti, Vietnam, Sri Lanka, and Ethiopia.

If you're thinking "what kind of play might I find in Ethiopia?," consider this fact.

Ethiopia's beer market is estimated to grow more than 10 percent per year until 2015. That demand should come from high GDP growth and bigger disposable incomes. Over the past five years, one company invested over $1.53 billion into its African business, which means it's ready to meet that demand. It's seen 11 percent increase in African sales. Now here's the best part: It's also ready to swallow up as much Latin American market share as it can. The name? Diageo Plc. You can find it listed on the NYSE.

The flipside of the consumption coin is debt, which we'll explore in the next chapter. History gives us a quick lesson, courtesy of David Graeber's book *Debt: The First 5,000 Years*.

Graeber spotlights the plight of the French colony Madagascar back in 1895. The French goal was the subjugation of the Malagasy: refugees and rebels from all over the Indian Ocean.

The French decided the best way to control the Malagasy were to get them addicted to imported luxuries. The idea was that consumer demand is the surest way to tie them to France. (They also decided to tax the heck outta them too, in newly-minted Malagasy francs.)

But, turns out, a bunch of locals were hip to the trap. They resisted. Graeber writes: "More than 60 years after the invasion . . . inhabitants would dutifully show up at the coffee plantations to earn the money for their poll tax, and then, having paid it, studiously ignore the wares for sale at the local shops."

Naturally, though, this form of protest didn't last above a hundred years. Guess who ended up in hock to the French?

Borrower beware.

My friend, resource investor Rick Rule drives the point home:

> We are now experiencing the impact of "moral hazard," where we subsidized damaging and irrational activities by the collective, by the financial services industry, and as individuals. In addition to encouraging these activities, we encouraged the mindset that it's the duty of society to compensate individuals and institutions for self-inflicted damage.
>
> Other parts of the world did not have our wonderful brand and franchise to devalue, and as a consequence they were forced to behave more rationally, Chile as an example is the

most solvent political entity in the hemisphere—
Keynsians who saved! Chinese workers save 40
percent of income! In a globalized economy,
we can't compete by consuming.

Amen, brother.

Chapter Four

Debts Do Matter

~

Borrowing, Borrowing, Borrowing

UNCLE SAM BORROWS 42 cents for every dollar it spends. We borrow about $4 billion a day. That's according to a one-month figure of $125 billion given by Treasury Secretary Tim Geithner.

How did we come to this? By the time we reached our 43rd president's term, the national government took leave of its financial senses and simply stopped paying for anything. Forget paying for two wars, tax cuts, or Medicare drug benefit.

Counting just the most recent and crisis-filled presidency, we've accumulated more debt in this period than we had from George Washington's day to the time that Bill Clinton scored his seat in the Oval Office.

The situation has never been graver.

Let's talk magnitude for a second. If Bill Gates gave every single penny of his fortune to the U.S. government, it would only cover the U.S. budget deficit for about 15 days. If Warren Buffett took over after that, he could float us another 13 days.

Or consider this charming gesture from a dead man in Coral Gables, Florida. He left his home and $1 million in cash to the government—for the purpose of paying down the national debt.

His 1929 Spanish style home—3,900 square feet, six bed/five bath, in need of "updates"—grossed $1.175 million at auction. The deceased's generosity won't go very far: Uncle Sam blew through his inheritance in less time than it took you to read about this—17 seconds.

Here's the deal: All that debt is manageable for as long as you can service it. That is, as long as Atlas' strength holds out, he can hold the world on his shoulders.

Right now, the dollar's strength depends on the reedy backs of politicians and Washington–Wall Street dealmakers who'll shift with every wind. They don't think long-term. They haven't been . . . not since the 1970s at least.

Servicing debt can be easy, so long as you can do so at a nice low rate. However, as we've seen recently with Greece, all it takes is a little political turmoil on the back of a lot of debt to spike borrowing costs up.

When you can no longer borrow at cheap rates, you start to run into problems. Usually your answer to retiring more debt is not to dip into some magic surplus of hard cold cash. Retiring debt happens when you take the proceeds from new, longer-term debt you're selling . . . or convincing everyone it's a great deal just to roll into more debt.

That works, for a while, the same way a gambler can go back to the same casino a bunch of times before he's finally thrown out.

Eventually, when your Treasury bond holders start to wonder where the next batch of money is going to come from, they demand higher compensation for holding the increasingly risky investment.

There's a reason why the treaty that all the EU countries signed made one important rule. They knew this government Ponzi scheme can't perpetuate forever.

So they laid down the law: Countries wishing to join the euro currency were not to have budget deficits exceeding 3 percent of GDP. And total government debt couldn't be higher than 60 percent of GDP.

Today, we see that no one's keeping that pledge. Not even stalwart Germany, the industrial backbone of the

Eurozone has managed that. And, surprise, surprise, guess who's having some trouble finding buyers for their debt these days.

We recently addressed a group of students at the Towson University school of finance. Our friend Tim Maurer (in addition to being a best-selling co-author of *Financial Crossroads*) teaches a class there on annuities and taxation—things that CPAs are supposed to know. After watching (we hope) the assigned prep, the documentary *I.O.U.S.A.*, Tim invited his students to bombard us with questions.

One hand shot up: "What is so bad about a debt-to-GDP ratio in the 90 percent range? We had greater ratios during and after World War II. And Japan has been running in excess of 130 percent of GDP for years? They seem to be doing fine."

"You don't know this yet," we tried to explain, "but when you leave school with a mound of debt, try to find work in a struggling economy—you'll begin to understand. When you try to buy a home . . . when you want to get married . . . send future children to school. When you try to hang your shingle and attract clients for your wealth advisory business, you'll begin to see that productive debt is not a bad thing. But unproductive debt, debt for consumption purposes, limits your options."

We used to be a nation of thrifty creditors. Now even our sharpest students look abroad and see no problem with collectivized risk and a mountain of unpaid liabilities.

Should it be a surprise, then, that these kids now graduate from college on average with a $25,250 debt burden? And what happens when they're seeing unemployment rates of 9.1 percent? They're certainly not the future consumers we're betting on to save America.

The situation is elementary. No one needs a college degree to know that our government can't keep acting like children who ought to clean their rooms.

Don't you always tell your kids, before they go outside to play: "Clean your room"?

And don't you always hear a 10-minute flurry of activity and then get an "I did," as you see a back heading out the door.

And don't you always discover that they've only stashed all their junk that was on the floor under the bed or into the closet?

When you open that closet, all the stuff comes tumbling out. . . .

What's correcting right now is a 60-year boom in credit that began after World War II.

At first, it seems really unfair. Here America has to economize (!)—maybe give up gewgaws and gadgets—while China starts snapping up Birkin bags and Bordeaux in record numbers. But then we realize we're all in the same boat over troubled waters, and some of us were unlucky enough to begin the race first.

∾

> We are in the closing chapters of the current Debt Supercycle, with different countries strewn out along the path, some at more advanced stages than others but all headed for a destination that will force major decisions if politically painful actions are not taken. The longer that process takes, the fewer options that are available and the more painful the outcomes.
>
> —*John Mauldin, January 7, 2012,*
> *"Thoughts from the Frontline"*

And It's Not Just the Government . . .

Downgrading is in a bull market. As this bull market proceeds, investors will return to a healthy admiration for the value of a cash-rich balance sheet . . . and will scorn the value of a government guarantee.

The near-extinction of the American AAA credit illustrates the point well. As you'll see, the government isn't the only one who is going the way of the dodo.

In the early 1970s, about 60 U.S. companies possessed a AAA rating. A decade later, that number had tumbled to 30. By the early 1990s, the ranks of AAA credits had dwindled to nearly 20. When the new millennium dawned, only nine AAA companies remained. Seven companies managed to retain this prestigious ranking until 2009, when Berkshire Hathaway, Pfizer, and GE slipped into the AA ranks.

Today, only four U.S. companies boast a AAA rating: Automatic Data Processing (ADP), Exxon Mobil (XOM), Johnson & Johnson (JNJ), and Microsoft (MSFT). And right now, they offer a yield equal or better to the 30-year Treasury bond.

The downgrade cycle is still gathering momentum. But the cycle is shifting from the corporate bond market to the government bond market—aka, the sovereign bond market.

Solution!

Dividend-Paying AAA Peers Are a Good Way to Generate Income, without Investing in Bonds

If you don't need to collect the income right away, you can bank it with shares of the Vanguard Dividend Growth Fund (VDIGX). Its top 10 holdings include all four of these AAA dividend payers: ADP, XOM, JNJ, and MSFT.

Many sovereign credits worldwide are struggling to maintain a semblance of creditworthiness, at least in appearance, if not in fact. But they are losing that struggle—Greece's Icarus-like plunge into junk status being the most conspicuous example.

The credit downgrades that are showering down on the sovereign borrowers of Europe and elsewhere are upending a generations-long belief that government bonds are safer than corporate bonds . . . and for good reason.

Debt Downgrades around the World

The history of sovereign finance is a history of broken promises. Governments are very good at stiffing their creditors.

During the boom phase of a lending cycle, creditors tend to forget this inconvenient truth. They forget that government borrowers are nothing like corporate borrowers. They forget that government revenues derive from confiscation, rather than production.

As a result, during the boom phase, creditors demand much lower interest rates from government borrowers than they do from similarly rated corporate borrowers.

During the bust phase, however, creditors start to remember how dangerous government borrowers can be. They start to remember that when times are tough, governments have a tough time confiscating enough national wealth to repay their bills.

Such is the predicament in which Greece finds itself today. But the Greek government is hardly unique. Greece may be the poster child of distressed sovereign borrowers, but its grim financial predicament is not so different from that of Portugal, Spain, Italy, or a dozen other sovereign borrowers around the globe . . . including the United States.

Now here's why I'd consider Johnson & Johnson over, say, a 5-year Treasury bond. The cost of insuring a 5-year Treasury note against default is now higher than the price of insuring a 5-year Johnson & Johnson bond against default. These insurance policies are called credit default swaps (CDS). And just like an ordinary insurance policy, the greater the perceived risk of an insurance claim, the higher the price of the insurance.

It may seem surprising that CDS buyers would consider Treasury debt riskier than J&J debt. But let's think about it this way. J&J is the 125-year-old AAA corporation that throws off $14 billion of free cash flow per year. The U.S. Treasury is the *222-year-old former* AAA federal agency that generates more than $1 trillion of *negative* cash flow per year. Which looks like a better deal to you?

In light of that comparison, the only surprise is that the prices of CDS on Treasury debt are not higher still.

A similar story unfolds in Europe. . . .

Consider Greece, Portugal, and Ireland. Two of those countries were triple-A credits one decade ago. All three of them now merit junk bond status.

Meanwhile, it now costs more to insure the AAA-rated bonds of the French government against default than to insure a basket of 125 European corporate bonds against default.

During the depths of the credit crisis of 2008–2009, the price of CDS on European corporate debt was more than double the price of CDS on French government debt. In other words, investors were much more worried about defaults by European corporations than they were about a default by the French government.

Today, however, the tables have turned. Investors now consider a default by the French government to be more likely than a default by the average European corporation.

This price trend does not suggest that a default by the French government is probable. But the price trend of French CDS relative to corporate CDS does suggest that a new phase of the credit crisis is under way.

On the other hand, take Brazil, Chile, and Colombia. These were all junk credits one decade ago. Today, they are all investment grade. Destiny, then, is not automatic. Governments of the Western world continue to pile up promises they can't possibly keep.

> ## SOLUTION!
>
> Consider investing in emerging market corporate bonds—or a fund that pools a bunch together. The key word is UPGRADES.

The Era of the Sovereign Default Is Now

Uncle Sam, for example, promises to police the world, to feed the jobless, to pay long-term Social Security benefits to retired folks, to provide universal health care for everyone, and to create jobs out of thin air—whether or not those jobs make any economic sense. The list goes on and on. One problem: Uncle Sam can't pay for any of this stuff unless he takes the money away from someone else.

The power of government relies on the power to confiscate: money, liberty, rights, property, dignity, opportunity, hope. . . . Eventually though, it starts to run out of things to confiscate.

We're seeing this, real-time, through the Occupy Wall Street movement.

The occupiers, broadly speaking, believe they have already lost most or all of their money, liberty, rights, property, dignity, opportunity, and/or hope. They believe they have little left to lose. More dangerous, they also believe they have much to gain by enlisting the government's power in redistributing some of the wealth owned by the "1 percent." The occupiers know that the 1 percent still has something to lose—something that the government could confiscate and send their way.

We don't foresee an "it's morning again in America" outcome. Here's the big problem: An alliance between disgruntled masses and a hostile government is not merely a threat to the 1 percent; it is also a threat to the very foundations of American enterprise. It is a threat to entrepreneurialism, to the pursuit of wealth and, yes, to job creation.

The government as an ally is about as reliable as a rabid pit bull. But in the midst of a revolution, there is little time for logic. Revolutions are about overthrowing the existing order in its entirety, even if large portions of the existing order are worth saving.

Therefore, a vicious cycle is under way. The more the crowds whine about lost opportunity, the more the governments—that is, the bankrupt agents of opportunity destruction—intercede. The more they intercede, the more they destroy opportunity and the more they bankrupt themselves.

These stories do not end well . . . ever.

The most reliable government guarantee of all is the guarantee that a government will attempt to abrogate its responsibilities and default on its promises.

Throughout the Western world, governments are struggling to confiscate enough wealth to repay their creditors. Meanwhile, many large corporations around the globe have never been in better financial shape in their entire corporate lives.

Consider the striking contrast between the debt levels of the U.S. government compared with the debt levels of the S&P 500 companies. One decade ago, when Clinton's crew was relishing America's last annual budget surplus, U.S. debt-to-GDP was floating around the 60 percent level. At that same moment in history, the debt-to-revenue of the S&P 500 companies was soaring to 90 percent.

Over the next six years, U.S. debt-to-GDP inched up to 66 percent, while the S&P 500's debt-to-revenue jumped to 111 percent! But then a funny thing happened . . . corporate debt levels plummeted, while Uncle Sam's debt levels soared.

The Crisis of 2008 pushed hundreds of billions of dollars of corporate debt into bankruptcy or onto the Federal Reserve's balance sheet, thereby producing the precipitous drop in corporate credit levels from 2007 to 2009. But since then, corporations have continued to retire debt and to bolster their balance sheets with cash.

> ### SOLUTION!
>
> Be choosy about corporate bonds. And be willing to look outside the United States.

Things Aren't Looking Good over in Muni-Land

Municipal finances in the various states of the union are also deteriorating rapidly.

These muni bonds fund everything from sewers to schools. Any infrastructure project happening in the state depends on this money as much as it does the handouts from the federal budgets.

Only nine states' general obligations earn a AAA from S&P.

What are the criteria? These are states who depend less on the federal government for their revenue and can balance their books well enough to weather federal funding cuts. (We wouldn't give overmuch attention to the rating itself . . . but we do consider their factors perfect checkboxes for your own list, should you decide to go the muni investing route.)

Meanwhile, dozens of states and local governments teeter on the verge of bankruptcy.

The worst case of 2011 was the capital city of Pennsylvania: Harrisburg. The state's ready to rush in and take over the city's finances. Meanwhile, Jefferson County, Alabama, filed the biggest muni bankruptcy filing in U.S. history. Cities like Providence, Rhode Island, and Detroit, Michigan, are poised to follow. Some black marks here are being in a state with the largest unfunded pension costs in the union or defaults on infrastructure bonds.

States like California and Illinois have hit rock bottom junk bond status. So we'd stay far away from them. Consider crossing New Jersey, Ohio, Michigan, Georgia, New York, Arizona, Connecticut, Ohio, and Florida off your list (unless you have a strong stomach and a brave eye for bargain hunting).

Why are they so badly off? Try the burden of paying off interest. Half of Nevada's budget goes toward debt servicing. Michigan's 40 percent. In Arizona, California, Connecticut, Ohio, and Illinois, debt payments now swallow over 20 percent of the budget.

Tax their way out of it? Well, there's a small problem with that—aside from sacrificing political popularity. Consider the Golden State for just a minute. There are more people unemployed in California than the entire population of the states of Nevada, New Hampshire, and Vermont put together. And housing prices have fallen in some hot spots by as much as 60 percent or more. That's a lot less wealth to tax!

So here's a rule of thumb: Watch out for states who can't balance their books with high correlation to housing price weakness, industrial weakness, Washington, D.C., dollars, or the Fed's bureaucratic spiderweb.

If I were you, I'd be a little worried about even *living* in one of these states. Take the second most dangerous city in America: Camden, New Jersey. In order to keep above the rising debt waters, they're shutting down half the police force. This all takes the prophecy "may you live in interesting times" a bit too far.

But we're not a total banana republic yet. If you're looking for some debt oases, Texas, Washington, Utah, and North Carolina look pretty solid.

When it comes to debt, the top five states with the lowest debt shouldered per person are:

1. Nebraska—$15
2. Iowa—$73
3. Wyoming—$77
4. South Dakota—$135
5. Arkansas—$312

Meanwhile, Connecticut, Massachusetts, Hawaii, New Jersey, and New York residents ultimately shoulder the most.

But that's not the only factor that matters, especially if you're someone living in one of these states.

Right now, when it comes to taxes and fees and cost of living—what it takes to pay for all that debt borrowing—some states are in a far worse-off place. I think you'll get the connection: Connecticut, Illinois, Rhode Island, Vermont, Minnesota, New York, and New Jersey. Minnesota, for instance has the fourth-highest income tax in the United States.

Consider even a less textbook perfect case.

You buy a house on the lake in Tennessee—there's no state income tax.

Tennessee looks very good on the debt list, at number 45. But for every $1 its residents and businesses send to Washington in taxes, Uncle Sam sends back $1.27 in benefits and programs.

That's testament to the bargaining power of Tennessee's congressional delegation . . . but what happens when Uncle Sam no longer has access to endless easy credit? Tennessee's a relatively small state. Not that many voters there. A presidential election probably won't hinge on Tennessee's 11 electoral votes.

The point is that in a crisis like the one that's looming, when politicians suddenly have a lot less money to dole out, some places are going to start looking expendable. Uncle Sam might very well tell Tennessee, "Sorry, you're on your own now."

Could Tennessee carry on with no state income tax if Washington told the state to fend for itself? Suddenly that fishing-hole lifestyle could become a lot harder to keep up.

So if you're about to retire or are planning to retire soon, consider these three factors if you're thinking you'll want to move.

Ideally, you want a state that:

1. Has total per capita debt below the national average of $1,297.
2. Sends more money to Washington than it gets back (or at least isn't too far out of balance the other way).
3. Has annual per household pension obligations below the national average of $1,219.

Considering just factor number three, you'll see that we're facing some big uphill battles as a nation. The unfunded pension liability tally for the 50 states stands at $3.2 trillion. Rhode Island is the state that shoulders the most.

And as you know, the feds aren't in a great position to dole out.

As federal stimulus monies run dry, expect more tax hikes on everything from income to booze. Expect more fees too, on everything from streetlights to fire hydrants. Then there are fines, like $191 for jaywalking in Los Angeles. The

DEBTS DO MATTER [67]

scramble for your cash is on: 36 of the 50 states have already hiked taxes and fees in the past two years.

While 2011 didn't prove the year that doomsayer Meredith Whitney predicted, $6 billion worth of muni defaults by 118 borrows is no slouch. There were 10 bankruptcy filings compared to just six the year before. The end of 2011 marked the twelfth consecutive quarter in which downgrades in the muni market outpaced upgrades, according to Moody's. The ratio is five downgrades for every upgrade—the worst since the 2008 crisis!

We predict that the easy budget cuts have been made, and that state and local finances will only face more hurdles ahead.

Once the preserve of widows and orphans, the muni bond market has become a game of chance that would feel at home on any casino floor—right between the craps table and the roulette wheel.

Things to Watch for . . .

Expect to see more muni defaults on a state-by-state basis. And brace your holdings for the domino effect. Many funds are required to invest in AAA-only securities. When downgrades happen, they'll be forced to liquidate holdings, and they'll have a hard time replacing that yield.

The deteriorating condition of government finances worldwide is causing an entire generation of investors to question the value of a government guarantee, at least in comparison to the value of a strong corporate balance sheet.

This loss of faith in a government guarantee is already forcing government bond yields higher in most parts of the globe. But the potential consequences of this lost faith extend far beyond the bond market.

If investors lose faith in sovereign debt, they are not far away from losing faith in all government guarantees, like the guarantee that a government will make good on its entitlement promises or on its verbal defenses to preserve the power of its currency.

In other words, the fissures opening in the sovereign credit markets signal the beginning of a tectonic shift in global finance—a shift that forces investors to select investments according to their real-world merit, rather than their government-contrived merit.

Once a government starts breaking its promises, all government guarantees are in jeopardy. That's brought even the biggest Treasury bond cheerleader to 'fess up.

Bond King Confessional

Bill Gross head of PIMCO—otherwise known as Pacific Investment Management—runs the world's largest bond fund.

In February 2011, he eliminated all Treasuries from the portfolio, only to miss the biggest Treasury rally since 2008. While he issued a mea culpa and added Treasuries back into the portfolio to the tune of 30 percent, he's making some pretty exciting claims about the new normal going paranormal.

He calls the world we're now in bimodal, and the things happening in Euroland are pure Ponzi scheme.

Italian banks fo°r instance are using LTRO (long-term refinancing operation) to issue state-guaranteed paper to get funds from the European Central Bank. Then they take the proceeds and put it into their own Italian bonds.

So Gross recommends only the cleanest dirty-shirt sovereign debts. What that means is that you want the cleanest balance sheets you can find. Go out as long as you can, since the yields on anything less than five years are practically nil. Going out long toward the 10-year range should be a better guard against that scourge: inflation.

Now comes the big catch: When the return on money becomes close to zero on the face of things—but negative in real terms—normal market functions may break down.

Right now we're seeing tens of thousands of layoffs in the banking sector. Banks have thrown branch expansion into reverse. Why? Because at near-zero levels they're still not making a good profit!

It's the result of life at the zero bound. Banks no longer worry about getting deposits because there's so little profit to be made from lending it back out. Extended maturities don't matter when they don't deliver extra juice to returns. Most of the proceeds are going nowhere but back into Fed reserves—not the commercial open market.

You see, the whole game of capitalism doesn't work with fed funds and 30-year Treasuries frozen at the same yield . . . especially not if corporate debt (remember those dwindling AAAs from earlier) gives about the same yield, too.

Finally, when the whole system no longer finds takers for the credit it creates, it'll deleverage.

Gross offers two safety valves for your portfolio.

When you buy corporate debt, don't dip below the A-ratings. In this environment, it's not worth the risk. Second, be sure to go senior, if you're buying bank debt. Don't risk being a subordinated holder. If something goes wrong, you'll want to be the first in line to be paid.

Watch Out!

You might think that the new financial reforms enacted in the wake of the 2008 crisis will help protect your portfolio's worth for you.

The sad truth is no. You have to take responsibility yourself! No fund manager or officer of the Comptroller of the Currency or the Fed Reserve will do it for you.

In fact, here's what's laughable about the reforms the famed Graham-Dodd legislation enacted. Before Graham-Dodd, banks depended on ratings agencies—Standard & Poors, Fitch, Moody's—to tell them which investment vehicles were risky and which weren't. Well, you see how well that worked!

The problem was old-fashioned conflict of interest.

Today, post–Graham-Dodd, we're still dealing with the same conflict. Only now, the conflict lies within and without. What I mean is that the most recent proposed rule suggested by the Federal Reserve, the FDIC, and the Office of the Comptroller of the Currency is to follow the Organization for Economic Co-Operation and Development (OECD). What the OECD says is safe, is safe for us! Keep in mind, though, the majority of the OECD, two-thirds, is made up of members from EU countries. They consider, of course, their sovereign bonds to be risk-free.

If you think this situation sounds like a replay of what happened with mortgage-backed securities and other bundled tripe, you're right.

The only other ruler of value and safety proposed by the new rulings is the internal models of the banks.

These, mind you, are the same schizoid banks whose models suggested housing values rising to the clear blue skies. They said that mortgage-backed securities helped diversify and diminish risk . . . while they secretly bet against the very same products they were selling to institutions who packed all their "safest" funds with these kinds of products.

Who got caught holding the bag? You.

(Continued)

> The rule here: know exactly what you own. No one has a bigger self-interest in the health of your holdings than you do.
>
> Portfolio managers are ready to collect the fees. Salesmen stand by for transaction fees regardless of what they're selling.
>
> Wall Street no longer cares as much about the client relationships as they did just two or three decades ago. You need to know what you're buying. Take charge of your fiscal fate.

We're sure your grandmother told you, neither a borrower nor a lender be. There's something to that adage. If you don't borrow, you're free. You don't owe anyone a darn thing . . . not a farthing. Meanwhile, if you're a lender, you're caged in by depending on what you loaned. You need to be repaid.

That's why anthropologist–debt specialist, David Graeber, hits the nail dead-on when he defines debt this way: "Debt is the perversion of a promise, a promise that has been perverted through mathematics and violence."

Think about it. Right now the mathematical perversions of debt have never been greater. It's been sliced and diced into so many forms and is held by everyone from here to Timbuktu. The threat of violence is always around the corner. And the domino effect is always a risk.

If one country defaults and quits the euro, for instance, why not more? Should Ireland's and Portugal's debt be restructured too? Will the Eurozone unravel? Anything is now possible. Be prepared.

Here's the five-stage cycle:

1. Value of the currency slumps.
2. Capital controls instituted.
3. Social collapse meets mass nationalization.
4. Huge losses for any company with operations in the country in question
5. Central bank can become insolvent due to the bonds it holds becoming near worthless.

Graeber is right to consider debt a method of conquest. It's a means of control, whether it be one nation over another, or one farmer in hock to the bank. And Graeber's horror is in the right place. After all, we're always paying for our own conquest. Chiefly, we pay in the form of tax.

Our nation raised a single powerful protest against this tax back in 1773—when it came from King George's crown. But you might say we're still paying for "colonial" debt today, every time we bail out another European bank.

We're certainly paying our due—and then some—by letting monetary policy be determined by the serial bubble blowers to accommodate the unbridled spending of our government. Consider the next chapter as an exploration of yet another hidden tax on your wealth.

Chapter Five

Inflation 101

∽

When Savers Get Punished

SINCE THE END OF 1999, the stock market has not come close to keeping up with inflation.

Now hold that thought, because we'll come back to it in a second.

Over the past year, an incredibly worrying trend emerged. No one is talking about it. The market cooled down, the Fed lowered expectations, but food and energy prices continued to rise. In fact, almost everything you can think of has been on the rise.

But the flat savings rate makes it impossible for us to keep up with this trend. Your money is shrinking in buying power each day.

The Daily Show proves a great ground for testing unintended economic consequences like inflation (so much so that we included a clip with Alan Greenspan in our documentary *I.O.U.S.A.*). Host Jon Stewart got Dr. Greenspan to agree that there's no such thing as a free market. Then Stewart ventures: "When you lower the interest rate and drive money to the stocks, that lowers the return people get on savings."

Dr. Greenspan: "Ah, yes indeed, yes indeed."

"So they've made a choice," says Stewart. "We would like to favor those who invest in the stock market and not those who invest in banks. That helps us."

"That, no . . . that's the way it comes out," says Dr. Greenspan, "but that's not the way it is."

So, bottom line, you're more likely to put your money into stocks, thanks to the Fed.

Say you wanted to play it safe, the way your grandparents and parents did and invest in a CD. From 2010 to today, we've seen CD rates hover just above the 0.5 percent mark. Meanwhile, the inflation rate has shot from just over 1 percent to 4 percent. (See Figure 5.1.)

By doing the right thing and saving, you're actually losing money. Sure, the balance stays the same and you

Figure 5.1   Creeping Inflation

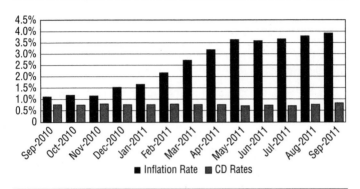

Source: Lifetime Income Report, Agorafinancial.com.

do get a token piece of interest, but you're not being rewarded, far from it.

Inflation's ugly work is quiet at first. Putting your cash in a bank at zero percent interest is like leaving an ice cube out on a picnic table. The longer you wait, the more it melts. If every year you're losing 3 percent or more thanks to inflation, that loss compounds.

You won't see it, of course, but that's what's happening.

Ultimately, the government dips into your bank account to pay down debt without your permission. Yet, this hasn't created a total bull rally, far from it. Instead, we're all just ambling along, waiting for something to shift.

You might say there are two types of inflation we're up against right now. First, there's price inflation. That's the kind you see every day, as you pay more for groceries, school tuition, health insurance, and the like.

The second—the real measure of inflation—is even more insidious. It's stealth. And it's brought to you by the central bank.

The real measure of inflation is the increase in the money supply. Chairman Greenspan, through his relentless cutting of interest rates, from 1996 to 2003, made it possible for banks to flood the worldwide economy with dollars. The money supply, as measured by a figure economists call M3, nearly *doubled* in that time.

The game continues today. They've more than doubled the money supply again—and in less time. And they're stepping up the pace. Since 2007 to today, the true money supply—according to the Mises Institute—has increased by $2 trillion. That's an increase of about $700–800 billion annually. That's about the amount of cash that the 500 stocks in the S&P were sitting on in 2011—their biggest cash hoard ever—while they didn't hire new workers.

What gives? Well, think about it. These corporations might not be simply greedy. They might actually be just that afraid of *another* perhaps even *bigger* economic bust ahead. This cash is basically earning a yield at or below inflation—just like your bank account.

These corporations aren't dummies. If you're a CFO at one of these blue chips, you went through a rain of brimstone and fire in 2008. That's why you'll continue to sit on a pile this large. You're not gonna get caught without a big cash cushion during what lies ahead.

Oh well, so much for the trickle-down theory of job creation and stimulus.

~

There are two things that can disrupt business in this country. One is war and the other is a meeting of the Fed Reserve.

—*Will Rogers*

Why are the feds doing this—if even business doesn't seem so confident? Because they need to monetize the government's vast debt. The only way the Fed can make this possible for Congress to spend beyond its means is by churning out more dollars in the money supply.

So it punishes savers with abysmally low interest rates and is ready to skewer older citizens living on fixed incomes. In turn, this monetary and interest rate policy discourages capital accumulation, small business creation, and entrepreneurs. The result? A weaker economy and a poorer America.

The Fed's inflationary policies may well hurt older people the most. Think about it. They rely on fixed incomes from pensions and Social Security, plus whatever savings they've mustered over the years. Inflation destroys the buying power of their fixed income and savings. The low interest rates reduce any income from their savings.

Meanwhile, younger people overborrow, because rates are so low. They don't even create savings to be eroded. And who can blame them?

When our own government doesn't worry about its debt burden, why should we? Well, because we're always the one paying the most for it.

Deflation, on the other hand, used to be called a good thing. Deflation in the realm of prices results from better technology, increased productivity, and price competition. Nobody complains when the price of gas, groceries, or their electricity bill drops, now do they?

Yet, the central bankers insist that a 2 percent inflation rate is exactly the medicine the economy needs to take every year—like an inoculation. Against what?

In fact, say we get that—2 to 3 percent inflation per year. Here's what happens to savers. The value of your savings will be halved in 15 years. In 30 years, you'd wake up and find those savings worthless.

That's why the interest rate matters so much. When the target interest rate is near zero, and the banks follow suit on your deposits, you just can't outpace this gentle menace.

Deflation Is Not a Dirty Word

Deflation is when prices fall. You'll see it come about frequently when credit or the money supply shrinks.

We declare deflation is not evil. And the central bankers are wrong to hate it. But let's examine their argument.

Deflation, they say, will cause people to put off spending! They say that if you see prices falling you'll wait to see them fall further. Hmmm. . . . We find that hard to believe. Computers have only gotten cheaper over the years, but that didn't mean we waited to equip the office until the iPad got cheaper. We gave iPads to everyone on our staff the year they came out.

In this case, as prices fall, more people can afford the product. And if they need it, they buy it. In an inflationary scenario—where the price of everything is climbing—you don't buy something when you need it. If you're scared the price will go up, you'll risk getting into debt just to beat rising prices.

In hyperinflationary situations, which you'll explore later, you'll buy *anything* because the value of your money is vanishing so rapidly. You'll buy anything that could be a store of some kind of value, because your money is not. In hyperinflation, prices can double in just a matter of hours. Store clerks can't even keep up! I bet you've heard the story about how a young gentleman in hyperinflationary Vienna orders a cup of coffee. An hour later he gets a second cup, at twice the price. The waitress then told him, well, if you'd wanted a second cup, you shoulda ordered it earlier. (Forget about the fact that it'll be cold). See how inflation monkeys with your purchasing decisions?

Likewise, some critics say that deflation punishes borrowers. Say you want to buy a big screen TV and a whole living room set. You take out a loan for the full cost: $1,179. But by the end of the year, both the TV and the furniture are worth less than your actual loan—which you are still paying off—$909. So you see, in this case, debt gets more expensive.

Imagine that! A world in which savers are rewarded, not borrowers and speculators. . . . Don't you think that might be a natural way to limit risk-taking in all sectors of the economy, from banks to house buyers? If we'd held to a more moderate monetary path all along, we'd have saved ourselves a heap of trouble.

Sure, the negative equity hangover that returning to sobriety creates is not fun. It will be painful. The thing is, we're running out of time: Stimulus in the form of dollars added to the money supply is giving us less juice for less time, each time we do it. That's unsustainable.

Since when did risk for risk's sake become a reward?

Again, it boils down to the ultimate fact that a government with massive debt will always like a little inflation to quietly erode the cost of that debt. No government wants the real burden of its debt to increase, just like the negative equity homeowner or the junkie who owes his dealer for the last fix.

Likewise, bankers tread a very thin line. Too much inflation and debtors repay loans in increasingly worthless money. Too much deflation and debtors will be more likely to default. The Federal Reserve wants to stay in the sweet spot.

———————————— ∼ ————————————

We had to wait five years. But it turns out our suspicion that the Federal Reserve is clueless, at best, is true. Newly released minutes from a January 31, 2006, meeting reveal that they laughed 45 times while they were about to be broadsided by the housing bubble. . . .
"We just don't see troubling signs yet of collateral damage, and we are not expecting much."

—*New York Fed chief Tim Geithner,
who now afflicts us as Treasury Secretary*
(continued)

"If I might torture a simile, I would say,
Mr. Chairman, that the situation you're handing
off to your successor is a lot like a tennis racquet
with a gigantic sweet spot."

—*Janet Yellen to Alan Greenspan*

While the *New York Times* called it a "lack of
comprehension" from "forecasting models that
turned out to be broken," we submit that the
problem is more basic: Hubris. Or, as Friedrich
Hayek called it, the fatal conceit.

Declining asset prices can ultimately be good for the
economy; they force people to invest well—not willy-nilly—
in only the most productive assets and companies.

And just to cap our point, let's take a quick peek at
some periods where deflation was good.

If you look at the period of deflation from 1866 to
1897, you'll see that the rate of economic growth was
perhaps the greatest ever experienced during so long a
period. Real GDP growth exceeded 4 percent per year.

But the comparison is a tricky one. Prior to 1914,
central banks rarely used monetary policy to stimulate
the economy. In that period, we were on a gold standard.

All these factors will impact how deflation treats us today.

Central bankers like to tell us there is only one kind of deflation: always bad. Economists like George Selgin are doing extensive research on the topic, and they conclude that there are two types of deflation: benign and malignant. The difference is in the cause.

The period from 1873 to 1896 was good to many Western nations. The gold standard, you see, placed limits on their ability to offset productivity improvements with monetary expansion. With their hands tied, prices declined. Scholars were ready to label this the first Great Depression, but they noticed something interesting: Every other economic indicator—wages, profits, industrial output, and trade—pointed to growth, even prosperity.

In fact, let's take a closer look. Two economists from UCLA and the University of Minnesota teamed up to check this twentieth-century phenomenon out. Andrew Atkeson and Patrick Kehoe looked at 16 countries in addition to the United States. They concluded that there were far more periods of deflation—enjoying reasonable growth—than there were depressions.

On top of that, Atkeson and Kehoe found that many more periods of depression were accompanied by *inflation*—rather than deflation. So deflation isn't the boogey man central bankers want you to think it is. In fact, the only episode that links deflation and depression is the Great Depression. (And that's after the Feds arrive on the scene in a big way . . . and Roosevelt goes on a spending spree.)

Often, legislators were the ones to cause downturns during the period with bad legislation. The idea is that if you keep central banks outta the equation, harm doesn't come from falling prices, so long as productivity gains remain in balance.

So in the 1990s we could have seen this happen again. After all, we did see massive gains in labor productivity, so the whole era we've just seen could have witnessed major reductions in the nominal cost of living. But that didn't happen. The central bank was tripping over its own feet.

One way to allow for "good" deflation would have been to target not consumer prices—as in the Fed mandate—but look to the growth rate of spending. Spending should grow at a rate equal to the growth of labor and capital. That could be about 2 percent. This would be a road with a few bumps. But as long as the Fed allows enough money out there to offset hoarding, you wouldn't see a 1930s-style crisis.

But here and now, the crisis may have gone too far. There's no way to avoid a much bigger crunch.

Ultimately your central bankers sold you down the river. You may enjoy *unpredictable* changes, which are worse than the predictable changes that happened during the pre-Fed Reserve era.

What *You* Need to Retire!

We didn't set out writing this book for the wealthy 1 percent. Far from it. But here's the reality. If you're going to live well, you'll have to become a millionaire.

I know it sounds crazy at first blush. But it's very possible. And it's never been more necessary to start thinking like you have a million bucks—doing what it takes to achieve it—rather than borrowing as if you have it.

Consider this basic formula. Say you start out earning $35,000 per year. That's not much. But if you save 12 to 13 percent, get a company match, and earn an annual raise of 3.5 percent or better, you can do it. What it takes is a 7 percent annual return to get you to a million dollars.

Now $1 million won't actually get you very far. Such a nest egg will give off $50,000 per year. That replaces 75 percent of income for someone making just over $66,600—satisfying the adviser's rule of thumb. You don't want to draw down more than 5 percent of the balance per year.

Add in Social Security's maximum (assuming that holds), and you'll get an additional $30,156 of income. Add that to the $66,000 and there's a total of $80,156—the recommended replacement for an income of $106,874.

But now get this: Medical expenses alone for a married couple entering their golden years are around $260,000. So you've got to plan for that. Meanwhile, most middle-income American Baby Boomers are sitting on a nest egg of less than $100,000.

Again, we can't stress this enough, there's no way that compound interest on savings accounts or CDs is going to cut it. Not while near-zero interest reigns.

You'll find more inflation-proofing solutions in the next chapter, where we'll offer advice on maintaining your standard of living. But for now. . . .

Five Quick Inflation-Proofing Moves for Your Portfolio

Here are five quick portfolio additions you can make to catch up and outpace the true bogey: inflation.

1. *Cash-rich companies.* Remember those stuffed-with-cash S&P companies earlier? Obviously, they're preparing for the worst. They also pay dividends, which helps cushion your return during times when share prices flatline or fall. (Should we enter a

period of deflation, a cash-rich company will still be your best friend. As a cash cow company will have little or no debt, it'll do better than the firms that borrowed heavily, or need to borrow. After all, its debt-laden competitors will be paying back loans with increasingly valuable dollars they'll wish they could spend elsewhere.)

2. *Stocks that hold pricing power.* Look for companies that can easily pass costs onto customers or end users. This especially applies to industries like health care and pharmaceuticals, chemicals, commodities, and consumer staples.

3. *Consider commodities.* Whether you add a few exchange-traded funds (ETFs) to your portfolio or select miners or buy options on commodities, this is an avenue that tends to do well as prices climb. If you had gotten scared after the first oil shock in 1973 and plunged into the Goldman Sachs Commodity Index, you'd have seen returns of 12.1 percent per year until 1981 versus average annual inflation of 9 percent. We already saw commodities protect investors in 2008, when prices of things like potash and gold went flying upwards. We'll see it again.

4. *Go for TIPS.* These are Treasury inflation-protected securities whose principal value adjusts to keep up

with inflation. This is a great option for fixed-income investors or those who have to go the 401(k) route and want added protection. Best of all, you can skip an extra fee by buying these directly from the Treasury. (That's the least they can do!)

5. *Foreign markets with raw materials*. As we pointed out above, producers of raw materials and commodities stand to benefit the most from inflation. Thus, nations that produce the most make natural hedges. Consider Canada, Australia, South Africa, or Norway when you flesh out the foreign equities holdings in your portfolio.

Chapter Six

Something's Gotta Give

~

Maintain Your Standard of Living

WAGES ARE FALLING—the real income of a typical American household is now below the level it was in 1997.

Since 2007, Americans' collective net worth has lost $5.5 trillion. That's an 8.6 percent drop that the Federal Reserve is willing to admit to. We've seen tallies closer to $7 trillion. What they don't 'fess up to is the creeping ways they've stolen your wealth.

Take consumer prices. The Bureau of Labor Statistics loves to massage the numbers.

Take January 2012, the year-over-year increase still looks ugly—3 percent. That's before all the geometric weighting, substitution, and hedonic adjustments.

Factor that out and report the number the way it was back in Jimmy Carter's day—what John Williams at Shadowstats.com does—and the real annual increase is 11.1 percent.

The government has been calculating the consumer price index since 1913. Each year, it starts to play more games. Consider this kind of thing, which is pretty small potatoes: The government assumes you'll switch from steak to ground beef and calls it even.

When you hear the reports, note what's left out. That's how the President in 2010 could claim the "lowest inflation rate in a decade"—he wasn't counting food or oil prices.

Consider a mixed basket of goods in 1790 cost you a hundred bucks. In 1913, you'd have paid a little more, $108. By 2008, you'd have to have forked over $2,422 for an equivalent basket.

But here's the real reason why you wouldn't count food or oil prices in the CPI. It comes down to two things: Social Security and COLAs.

COLA isn't a carbonated beverage, but it is the magic Kool-Aid your government gives you to sit down, shut up, and collect your Social Security check in relative peace.

The COLA—cost of living adjustment—came about (surprise, surprise) in 1975. Naturally, if you're a senior living on a fixed income, or someone who's about to live on a fixed income—namely, Social Security—you're condemned to get less and less, if the fixed payment isn't adjusted. Hence the COLA.

To calculate the COLA, the government uses the CPI index. Now I'm sure you can guess why they doctor the CPI.

Right now, we've hit a crucial point.

For the first time since the Great Depression, U.S. households as an aggregate are collecting more money in payments from the government than they're paying in taxes.

Households paid $2.2 trillion in tax year 2010. But, when you tally up everything from Social Security to unemployment benefits, to Medicare and Medicaid, to veterans' and other cash transfers of government dole, Americans receive $2.3 trillion.

Obviously, something's gotta give. While we'd say the first step is to spend less, that's not how the government thinks. They'd rather find ways to play out the charade.

That includes making the CPI smaller than it is—thus cutting the amount of reasonable COLA they'd have to add on to these entitlement payments they make.

Now they'll argue that they cut food and energy prices out of the CPI because it's "volatile." Sure it's volatile, but it's no less a factor in the average American's quality of life.

Here's just a quick example of the kind of games afoot here.

Remember that temporary Social Security tax cut that Congress and the White House came to a head about at the end of 2011? You might recall the payroll tax was trimmed two percentage points for 2011 . . . for what were touted as its stimulus effects. The president described it as "a tax cut that economists across the political spectrum agree is one of the most powerful things we can do to create jobs and boost economic growth."

Where did it go? It all went into the gas tank. The typical U.S. household spent $4,155 on gasoline in the past year. That's an 8.4 percent chunk of the family's income—the highest since 1981, according the Oil Price Information Service.

Over the past decade that chunk was only around 5.7 percent. So that's a difference of $1,300. Meanwhile, if we look at median family income, according to Census data, it's $49,445.

Do some back-of-the-envelope math . . . that income's payroll tax trimmed from 6.2 percent to 4.2 percent . . . and it works out to $989.

So for the typical American family, every penny of the payroll tax cut has been eaten up by higher gas prices. And then some.

This CPI-jiggering is just the start of things to come. In Chapter 5, we already covered how the central bank's policies can wipe out your account's worth in as little as three decades.

Maintain Your Standard of Living—Despite the Central Bank

Have you noticed life is not as good as it used to be? If you're reaching deeper into your wallet to buy the same old things, you're not crazy.

In fact, the average American's standard of living has tumbled more sharply in just the three years since the 2008 crisis than it has than any time since the United States started keeping track in the 1960s.

Said average American has $1,315 less to spend since the start of the Great Recession.

Let's review. The cut to our standard of living comes from a three-one punch:

1. Stagnant incomes
2. Price inflation
3. Falling net worth

If you consider the unemployment rate alongside inflation—the Misery Index—we're at our highest level of misery since 1983.

What follow are some great ways for you to fight back and keep misery at bay. In fact, we think you can use these tips to build your wealth in the years ahead.

Try This Anti-Inflation Play

Worried about rising food costs? We are. Why not profit from it? Investing in grocery stores isn't necessarily the way to go. They generally have high input costs and low margins. In other words, they are very poor income payers.

But there is an alternative.

Instead of investing in the low margin side of the food trade, you should follow the money upstream. Forget transportation, food products, or even seed and fertilizer. One of the best ways to make money in any industry is by investing in the tools of the trade, rather than the trade. We're talking farm equipment.

Rising food prices have put a little extra cash in farmers' pockets. Or at the very least, they have incentivized farmers to increase crop yield. To do that, they need more equipment.

Likewise, if you're worried about higher oil and gas prices ahead (Strait of Hormuz excitement aside), there are plenty of great ideas to explore.

Even if you're paying more at the pump and paying more to heat your house or paying more for your electricity, you can get some of that money back, and then some, by investing in the companies that most stand to benefit from those higher costs.

For example, avoid refineries, but do consider a bevy of oil and gas exploration firms. The smaller they are, the better. As good deposits of monstrous size are becoming rare, the only way the big firms like Exxon keep up their reserves is to snap up younger, more nimble firms that take the risk to find good deposits. They'll often buy out these companies at a premium delivering you the gains.

But there's far more to be done! Of all the victims in the Fed's maw, the generation that's about to retire will be hit the most. Boomers, this section is for you.

Phase III Retirement Investing

Whatever is left of the baby boom generation's retirement is about to get wiped out. It's the third and final step in the systematic destruction of a whole generation's wealth. Okay, bold statement . . . we agree. But hear us out.

The first step came with the dot-com crash. Retirement accounts stuffed with tech stocks pumped by CNBC—or funds that bought tech stocks pumped by CNBC—were vaporized. Our intrepid Boomers picked themselves up, dusted themselves off, and a few years later they figured they were riding high again.

Yes, their retirement accounts were a shadow of their former selves, but their homes were rising in value 10 percent a year, every year.

Then Phase II hit. The Federal Reserve encouraged folks to load up on ARMs. The Fed Chairman assured us there'd never been a sustained nationwide drop in home prices. We know how this one ended, too. In their effort to chase yield, bankers on Wall Street created the Frankenstein known as mortgage-backed securities (MBS) and went on to insure them with the abominable credit default swap (CDS). That derivative stew poisoned the entire global financial system. Now comes Phase III. Baby Boomers are approaching retirement age.

What are you supposed to do with whatever wealth you have remaining? Why, unless you're a speculator in stocks and commodities and willing to bet on monetary policy outcomes, you're supposed to play it safe with fixed income, of course. What is first and foremost? U.S. Treasuries.

A 10-year U.S. Treasury note yields a paltry 1.85 percent as we write. Consumer prices—even using the government's heavily gamed figures—grew 3 percent over the last 12 months.

In other words, if you lend your money to Uncle Sam in "safe" Treasuries, you lose all of your yield, and a bit of your principal, to inflation. It's even worse if you opt for a savings vehicle like a bank CD. The best rate we find for a 5-year CD on the Internet is 1.95 percent.

This is no accident. It's policy (even if, in the end, we discover it is accidental policy). "Negative real interest rates" are how the federal government will try to pay down some of its staggering debt.

This puts income investors in a real pickle. Sure, they could turn to a corporate bond fund. That's tricky, though, when the economy is slowing and profits are bound to come in below Wall Street's lofty expectations.

Of course, there are municipal bonds, and the tax advantages they bring. But at a time when municipal budgets are strained and whole cities in California are filing for bankruptcy, how "safe" is that?

Income investors need to throw out the traditional playbook . . . and pursue alternative income strategies.

For instance, did you know you could take a humble corporate bond yielding 7 percent, collect a yield of 10 percent, and cash out a 73 percent gain? And all without adding risk or leverage?

Consider Company X for a second. Let's say it's expanding its business, planning to open 10 new stores.

To do so, it issues 5-year bonds, called notes, with a 7 percent coupon rate.

Say that in year number two, its industry hits a downturn. While sales growth slows, the company is still raking in steady cash flows. However, investors are worried, and they sell their bonds. Prices fall from their $1,000 par value to $700. This is where you can step in.

If you run the math, and discover that even with the slowdown, the company can still pay off its bondholders, you should buy. The sell-off offers locking in at an even-lower bond price.

At $700, that 7 percent coupon rate actually pays 10 percent ($70 annual interest divided by your $700 investment). Plus, in just three years, you'll receive the full redemption price of $1,000.

You'd receive six $35 interest payments semi-annually, totaling $210 for the three-year period. That brings your total return to $510. We put down only $700. So in three years, we cash in a 73 percent gain, or 24 percent annually.

Your broker won't tell you about this strategy, because there's little in the way of fees to collect.

Here's another tack, albeit one of the more aggressive strategies we'll mention here: This one allows you to double or triple your stock dividends, again without adding risk or leverage. It involves three steps as follows. Best of all you can do this with stocks you already own:

- STEP No. 1: You buy a stock.
- STEP No. 2: A speculator pays you an upfront fee for the future option of purchasing your stock at a higher price than you paid for it.
- STEP No. 3: You pocket that fee (called a premium) and sit on your shares like you normally do. You *never* have to pay this fee back—no matter where the stock goes in the future. It's yours to keep . . . forever.

Following this strategy, our resident Agora Financial income expert, Jim Nelson, unearths yields in excess of 19 percent. Jim only considers the safest blue chips in the market.

This brings us to some larger questions. Even if you do smart things, how can you be sure the government doesn't get more aggressive and seize your wealth in other ways. The longer you wait to protect your money, the fewer solutions there are!

Is My 401(k) Safe?

Argentina, about 10 years ago today, experienced one of the worst post-war monetary crises. Not only did they default on debt and devalue the currency, they nationalized pension assets. They even closed the banks!

Folks were eager to get whatever cash they could scrape together in whatever form they could over the border to keep their savings safe. They smuggled it in rowboats into Uruguay.

Similar things can happen here. That's the catch. Capital controls can enslave your money and keep it within borders. The worse things get, the more troubled governments hate that you and your dough can escape.

I suggest you take action. You still have a shot to get plenty of money out. Things are pretty open for now, but I guarantee you, that when the gates close, they'll shut with a clang, and who knows when they'll open again?

Is My Bank Safe?

Like we've said earlier, everything that happened in the last crisis still lurks around the corner to be dealt with again. The purpose of much of the emergency lending facilities and bailouts wasn't to clean up the banks' act or get more jobs for citizens who want to work. Bernanke was happy to declare quantitative easing—that is, money printing—a success when stocks began to climb.

But bank stocks didn't get to rally for long, and some are still seething in toxic waste. Bank of America, slipping under $5 as we write, doesn't look like it has what it takes to survive.

In fact, if you consult recent CMA data and credit default swaps pricing, there's a 1-in-5 chance that Bank of America will default in the next five years. Old Pierpont Morgan's namesake is right there along with it. Those are bad odds.

Add to that what could be the biggest financial explosion on earth: The four largest U.S. banks—those most levered—are sitting on about $249 trillion in financial instruments tied to the European banking sector. Those are things like credit default swaps that they'll have to pay should any of the Eurozone nations default.

And keep in mind that the euro banks are leveraged to the hilt from gorging on sovereign debt. They hold 30 times as much sovereign debt as they do capital. Sure not all of it will default, but all it takes is a nation or two to start a crisis that ripples throughout the entire global finance market. We've seen it happen time and again (as we'll cover in more detail in Chapter 8).

It's best not to have all your eggs in one basket with any of the big banks. Our colleague and friend Chris Mayer does work on the banking sector (and is a former investment banker himself), and he has identified five savings and loans he considers safe. These modest, successful banks aren't only a safe place to stash money—he believes they'll even make good investments.

SOLUTION!

You Can Still Make Safe Money in the Much-Hated Banking Sector

It's the little guys—small, traditional thrifts—that are stuffed with the most cash. Our favorites are recently converted thrifts.

The trick is that when these private thrifts go public, they raise a bunch of cash, yet they usually trade at discount to book value. Such thrifts walk around with targets on their backs. By law, they cannot be acquired until three years after they convert. Statistically, about half of them do get bought out within three to five years at a premium to book value. Currently, takeout premiums run around 110 to 120 percent of book.

Joe Stillwell of Stillwell Partners has been active in this area. "What we're seeing now is almost too good to be true," he told *Grant's Interest Rate Observer.* "Clean, overcapitalized thrifts, with less competition than they've seen in years, are coming public at less than one-half of their value to private buyers."

Chris Mayer has more of his money in recently converted thrifts than any other investment idea. And he keeps buying: "I can't help it," he says, "It's like candy to a value guy. And even though bank stocks are down this year, my thrifts are up, easily beating the market—and doing so with much less risk than investing in the market."

These are nice, relatively safe places to invest and can give you some balance to your portfolio for those nail-biting days when everything is in the red. If you don't take Chris's word for it, try legend Peter Lynch:

> Pick five S&Ls that fit the Jimmy Stewart profile, invest an equal amount in each of them and await the

> favorable returns. One S&L would do better than
> expected, three okay, and one worse, and the overall
> result would be superior to having invested in an over-
> priced Coca-Cola or a Merck.
>
> —*Peter Lynch,* Beating the Street

Consider banks like Peoples Federal Bancshares or Fox Chase Bancorp.

Why You Might Try a Shari'ah Bank

I know this next one might sound really crazy to you, but hear me out. After all, it's not like you have to bank in Iran to make this work. Try Jakarta or Singapore, places where British common law still keeps order.

Shari'ah banking ethics came to be in order to comply with the Koran's laws against usury and other similar practices. So for example, say you want to buy a Rolls Royce. Instead of lending to you directly and charging you interest, a Shari'ah bank will buy the car for you, and sell it to you in installments at a higher price than they paid. That's how to get around interest.

But here's what really matters. Shari'ah banks are criticized for doing too much plain vanilla lending. To my mind, that sounds like a big positive. In fact, the bank treats its account holders like shareholders. They'll keep your money safe, and they'll give you a share of the profits in lieu of interest. When it comes to lending, the bank and entrepreneur both share the reward and failure. That's not like your typical big Western bank like Bank of America that can slice and dice every loan and parcel it into derivative sausage.

After all, profit and loss are the most efficient regulators. This injunction against interest also keeps Shari'ah banks from dealing with the central banks when it comes to emergency lending windows and the like—all the offerings (read: bailouts) that have kept the poison directly on the books of all major U.S. banks—or worse—transferred them right onto the government's balance sheet.

Now, for the best thing of all: capital requirements. Capital requirements are the amount of assets the bank has in reserve to cover paying out money to its deposit holders and to cover potential losses on investments of every stamp and flavor.

Our banks have squeaked by their regulators carrying dismal ratios. Try 1 and 2 percent of assets. Now, after the big Basel meeting of Economics' supposed brightest bulbs, the new capital requirements will be a total of 8 percent. That's the new "stiffer" regulation. And get this, Basel has given banks an extra seven years to make that happen. Banks won't have to be well-capitalized until 2019.

Meanwhile, Shari'ah banks already surpass those new "strict" capital requirements. They demand that their banks keep 12 percent asset backing at all times. So regarding some accountability of assets, Shari'ah banks already have the rest of the global banking system beat.

While we wouldn't dream of promising a Shari'ah bank is free from collapse risk, we will say that there are some huge points in its favor when it comes to capital. It's worth investigating further depending on where you live and how much money you're looking to protect.

What About Retiring Overseas?

We'll get into specific currency winners in Chapter 10, but it's worth pointing out that retiring overseas can be a great way to stretch your dollars farther and make your retirement years the best of your life.

We have a few ideas on places we like that we've visited: Medellín; Colombia; or León, Nicaragua. And we've spent plenty of wonderful December weeks in Nicaragua at Rancho Santana (think Big Sur at half the price).

The more wealthy and active entrepreneurs in the world we meet—everywhere from Singapore to Dubai—the more convinced we are that becoming a Penthouse Gypsy will be the norm rather than the rule if you want to live well, make money (and keep it).

We wonder if this won't happen to our country: that the most intelligent and productive people will just pick up and move. There's every reason to expect an *Atlas Shrugged* scenario when the top minds in production, manufacturing, and transport simply go on strike and vanish.

Our government is afraid, just like the government in Ayn Rand's America. While they've not made it illegal for you to retire, quit your job, or sell your business, they do make it harder to disappear.

∿

One Reader Says It's Happening: The Exodus of the Productive

My beloved wife and I attended an *International Living* conference in Las Vegas to explore living outside the country of our birth. I am beginning to see a light at the end of the tunnel. Our business interests in Russia and Hong Kong are expanding and I intend to close my business in America completely by the conclusion of the first quarter. My wife and I have selected a property to move ourselves and our four-legged children to in Central America.

We have chosen a country, after a great deal of research, which has no central bank and is relatively secure. The main reason we chose this particular country in which to establish citizenship is the tax structure for income earned outside the country.

It is hard to believe that America is driving away the entrepreneur to the point that I know I am not alone as a self-made man amongst many who have given up on trying to change the system in America. I am truly astonished sometimes at the extent of my network of friends who are also looking to "get out," and soon.

—"Daily Reckoning" *reader, John Z.*

Speaking of making it harder to disappear, passports, we note, came to be thanks to wars. When seafarers made world trade go round in the 1600s you needed "sea letters" to grant safe passage, as war ever-threatened the flow of goods and people.

World War II cemented passports' necessity in our lives. Post-9/11, we see them take on an even larger role. The passport is a great way for the state to control not only your person, but your property as well. And that definitely includes your cash.

There are a lot of exiles in this world. Each one has his own reason; we have ours. Long before we left America, the America we knew left us. We travel not to get away from it, but to find it.

—*Bill Bonner, "Exiles Eternal," July 2006*

Today, the United States is the only developed country taxing its citizens regardless of where they live. In fact, they're even taxing incomes of people who didn't even know they're citizens!

Most countries in the world simply tax people on where they live and work.

The most outrageous U.S. taxation case is one where you're an accidental U.S. citizen. That is, you were born overseas but had at least one U.S. parent. It doesn't matter that you never set foot on U.S. soil. You're supposed to file a tax return.

Ridiculous? Yes. But fortunately, the Tax Code contains an escape clause.

You can earn up to $92,900 per year tax-free (as of 2011) if you live and work outside the United States. If your spouse accompanies you overseas, double this exemption. So jointly, you can earn up to $185,800 annually, free of U.S. income tax obligations. You can also exclude or deduct some of your housing expenses from your gross income earned abroad.

Many of our readers write in to tell us that they believe in getting out of Dodge. However, unless you do it right, there can be a tax nightmare. If you fail to file your disclosure of foreign bank accounts, you could pay a fine of $10,000. That's a lot of work, the tax prep alone could cost you thousands per year.

However, the reward still tempts. In the year just after the 2008 crisis, the number of citizens choosing to expatriate jumped some 300 percent. And it continues to climb. Over 6.4 million Americans live overseas. That's only an estimate. The State Department only tallies from those Americans filing a tax return on overseas income. Many living abroad don't. As long as they don't try to return to the United States for a visit, they're off Uncle Sam's radar.

More are even willing to take the extreme step of giving up their U.S. citizenship. During the first half of last year, 1,018 did so. The number for all of 2010 was 1,534, so pending the final numbers, 2011 is on pace to exceed the previous year's record.

In many cases, citizenship renunciation is a good solution for people who have a lot to lose in taxes. Of U.S. citizens who get second passports, 58 percent eventually renounce U.S. citizenship.

Some other options for U.S. citizens:

- Canada
- Chile
- Australia
- New Zealand
- Austria
- Ireland

- Great Britain
- Dominica
- St. Kitts and Nevis
- Hong Kong
- Brazil
- Singapore

What differs from locale to locale?

First, the amount you'll have to spend. It may or may not be refundable.

Second, some take longer than others to set in motion—especially the more complex, which require land or real estate investment.

Third, there are differences in hurdles to jump after you've made the necessary local investment.

We're not saying you should expatriate or that there's no solution but to revoke your citizenship. But we'd like to point out, if something really bad happens here, it could be too late.

It's like trying to apply for flood insurance *after* Hurricane Katrina destroys your house. You buy insurance for your car, your house, your health, even your life. So buy insurance for *your way of life*. This is just another way to protect your assets. It's not a declaration saying you hate America.

It takes time to put together genuine documents, but that's not the only reason you'll have to hurry.

First off, depending on the country, it takes as much as a decade to realize the full tax freedom and benefits. For example, if you're interested in Hong Kong, Singapore, New Zealand or Chile, the residence and naturalization process could take as little as two years, or as long as seven.

Hong Kong at present takes seven, which you can establish via a work or investor visa. Singapore is the most generous, where citizenship can be had in just two. Chile or New Zealand will take five years.

Why do we like Asia? If you have residency in one of the Asia-Pacific Economic Cooperation (APEC) countries, you can get visa-free travel throughout Asia.

The APEC Business Traveler Card (ABTC) is a small plastic card that entitles you to visa-free travel for at least 59 days. Plus you'll enjoy fast-track clearance at airports and other ports of entry. That means priority clearance at customs, immigration, check-in, and security.

This is especially nice as China and Vietnam have pretty intense visa processes, so your travel freedom will do you good here.

It's no wonder that Jim Rogers took the family away from New York City and brought them to Singapore. He sees making the Asia move today as the thing that will ensure his heirs are wealthy in 2100. Just as the United States circa 1900 was a good move, or UK circa 1800 was the place to start a dynasty of wealth. Time to teach your kids Mandarin!

Second: The cost of disappearing is getting even more expensive. If you want to get a second passport, it'll likely cost more in this year than it did before.

For example, consider St. Kitts and Nevis (about an hour's flight from Puerto Rico). St. Kitts is raising the price of its passport by $50,000. However, the benefits are great. If you're in business, the visa-free travel to more than 90 countries including Canada, the UK, Switzerland, and Sweden, will stand you in great stead.

The real estate you buy there is great for future retirement. And before that happens, you can enjoy collecting solid rental income as people flock there for warmth between December and March.

We admit this is a costly move. You'll have to buy $250,000 in real estate to qualify. But, after you purchase the property, you'll find your citizenship could come through in as little as four to eight weeks. Dual citizenship is no problem in their minds, and your new St. Kitts and Nevis citizenship won't be reported to your home country.

Again, you shouldn't wait to act.

The list of countries that offer legal, fast legitimate second citizenship and second passports is shrinking fast. Countries like the United States with high taxation levels are making countries that offer this out feel the heat. Already the citizenship programs in Belize and Granada have been suspended for an indefinite period. Who knows when the doors to citizenship in Dominica or St. Kitts and Nevis could swing shut?

I have also left the USA, and am now living in Ecuador . . . I am surprised that none of your readers mentioned health care as a reason to leave.

In America, workers are held hostage to jobs they hate because working independently or taking early retirement means no access to health care unless you are willing to pay a thousand dollars a month for insurance. International health insurance costs me less than $100 a month.

—*"5 Min. Forecast" reader responds to "America: Love It or Leave It?"*

The United States Wants to Keep You as a Milk Cow

Nota bene: The United States isn't happy about your leaving the states of the Union, and they will make a last grab for your cash. It's called the exit tax, enacted in 2008. It's a tax on the capital gains of assets held since you've acquired them—as if the sum total is this year's income.

These assets are taxed "as if those assets are being sold"—even if you have no intention of selling them. However, it does not apply if your net worth is less than $2 million. Work it, if you're so inclined.

One reader, an expat in Germany, wrote us:

> In my case, before expatriating, I had sold a company a couple years before, paid taxes on the gain in that year (15 percent) to Uncle Sam and had only minimal additional gains since then. The exit tax will be on those small gains since I sold the company, not on all the gains from the sale of the company itself (which would, in fact, be double taxation).
>
> If you have a house you bought 20 years ago and it's appreciated five times even after the recent declines, yes, you would owe long-term capital gains on that house. That

could be a problem if you can't raise the cash for the taxes otherwise or can't sell the house.

If you are small fry . . . my recommendation is like the Nike ad—"Just do it." It's a very liberating experience.

Offshore Trusts Aren't Just for Big Corporations

Hand in hand with these kinds of offshore moves, you can set up a foundation holding ownership in an international business corporation (IBC). In this scenario, the designated protector, and any beneficiaries he or she chooses, can all participate 100 percent anonymously. The foundation is a holding company for a corporation.

The IBC benefits from being tax-free in its location (e.g., Antigua, Seychelles, Dutch Antilles, the Virgin Islands) and is able to give you privacy when it comes to present and future investments.

Plus, your heirs will reap the big gains. Forget worrying about what goes on in the United States over estate taxes. Since your offshore trust allows the inheritance to come from outside the United States, the assets are not prey to the usual taxes and legal procedures.

Through your foundation, your heirs get their inheritance free from probate, estate tax, gift tax, inheritance tax, or legal delays.

But if going abroad simply isn't for you, what's to be done?

Two Big Inflation-Outpacing Investments for Whatever the Future Holds

This might cause you to do a double take, but, buy a house! If you can afford it, buy two.

What? I hear you say, "Weren't you just telling me that buying houses was what got the bubble going in the first place?" True. But here's the catch.

If you're going to outpace inflation, the best thing you can do is put dollars into hard assets. Houses are hard—and rentable—assets. So is farmland. We like both in times of inflation.

The catch: only buy what you can afford. We're not talking house-flipping here. What you want to do is buy and hold . . . and hold some more.

Let's look back to our last big inflationary period: the 1970s.

Say you bought a modest single family home in 1972 for $30,000. Just three years later—after inflation rates spiked to 12 percent—you were sitting on a $39,000 home. By the end of the decade, the net worth of your house had more than doubled to $64,200.

Farmland too, offers a great inflation hedge. You might say farming is the only ever-growing industry by demand. You can cut back on a lot of things, but eating is the sterling human need. And as countries around the globe have population explosions, regardless of economic conditions, we'll need more food.

Consider just the tough times of 2008. Farmland returned investors 15.8 percent—trouncing both S&P returns and inflation.

Going back over the long haul there have only been two brief occasions when farmland offered negative returns: the 1930s and the 1980s. Looking at its performance from 1941 to 2002, average farmland values have inflation beat by 2 percent.

If we look at just the 1970s again, here's what farmland did. The investor who put all his money in the S&P 500 lost half. The investor who put his dollars into farmland was up 176 percent.

Better still, farmland offers something that physical gold sitting in the safe can't: cash flow!

Interested? You needn't go to a local auction or strap on some overalls and start farming. A simple place to start is a fund that pools farmland investments.

You can't get more basic than American Farmland Company with farms from the Corn Belt to the Pacific Coast. We've also been hearing about some new opportunities opening up for non-Canadian investors in Canada.

After you consider the case studies in the next chapter, you'll see why the prospects of Canadian farmland have us stoked.

A Tale of Two Deficits

Answers for the United States

AS YOU'RE FINDING OUT, currencies in trouble are nothing new. We've been confronted throughout history with massive currency crises, and we've always been able to deal with the fallout. Whether you're a Goldman Sachs trader in Singapore or a gaucho in Argentina or a garbage man in France, there are plenty of steps to take, but the biggest steps are usually in government's hands to make.

Our current fearless central banker Bernanke earned the nickname Helicopter Ben for a reason. He said that when times got tough, you could just throw down cash on the strapped populace from a helicopter to aid recovery. While he calls himself a student of the Great Depression, he's as much a student of the kind of work that created the great stagnation that Japan's been enduring for years.

It used to be that if you wanted a stellar example of post-war prosperity, Japan was your *Time* magazine spread. This nation made the best of its post-war peg to the dollar and innovated and exported its way to prosperity.

It had everything: good work ethic, competitive spirit, and a nation of savers. Really there was just one problem: deficit spending. It's not the way to grow an economy. As we'll see with Japan, it's a great way to destroy it.

The Yen Miracle as it was called, lost its luster in 1997. It proves that weak economies have weak currencies and strong economies have strong currencies. But a strong economy may not perhaps a strong currency make.

The Myth of the Yen Miracle Revealed

By 1997, Japan was in deep trouble. The brakes began squealing on its years of growth—GDP growth—or as I like to put it, growth domestic deceit. You see, the government was mounting ever-higher budget deficits. Realizing it had to do something and fast, the government made modest cuts, resulting in economic free fall. Productivity? Growth? All slowed. Inflation ran up.

Worse fuel on the fire: Housing prices started falling in 1991 (and kept falling for the next 13 years straight).

Worried politicians wrung their hands. What can we do but spend to fix this ugly economy? But in 1998, things just got worse by all measures.

Between 1992 and 1999, the Japanese government launched 10 financial stimulus packages, and debt grew by $1.13 trillion. (In our latest crisis, our Federal stimulus packages took a similar tact, with gargantuan sums. Our Troubled Asset Relief Program (TARP) alone cost $356 billion, of which $118.5 billion has been paid back. The government spent more than $577.8 billion on things like the Cash for Clunkers program, tax relief, and other economic stimulus measures. Our Federal Reserve plunged $1.5 trillion into various credit facilities and bailouts, as well as debt and bond purchases.)

The real cost of financial stimulus is on full display here. Japan's ratio of government debt to GDP soared from 60 percent in 1992 to 105 percent of GDP in 1999. You just can't spend your way out of trouble!

Here's the kicker, when you stimulate with money you don't have, which demands more debt, you never see debt reduction. If you backstop your banks and other enterprises with cheap credit, you don't get deleveraging. You get the opposite. Is Mr. Bernanke paying attention yet?

Moving debt around and changing its face doesn't fix the problem of deficit spending. The U.S. Fed has not yet learned this. Yet conditions in Japan in the 1990s are very similar to conditions in the United States today. It's a mistake for policy makers to believe the outcome will be different here.

While our ever-falling economic indicators seem to notch down the dollar's value gradually, we're now seeing federal budget deficits climbing sky-high, and the dollar is weakening.

Japan's nation of savers is happy to gobble up its massive government debt. Only 5 percent is owned by foreigners, which is why you'll never hear of China threatening to dump its JGB holdings; they're hardly holding any.

But, we admit, Japan is a paradox. Its 15-year-old zero interest rate policy has yet to charge life into its chronically weak economy. Yet, its credit growth is the slowest in the world. It's still the world's third-largest economy. When the government unleashes money into the public sector, it sees the Nikkei recover—until they turn off the tap. You can see that relationship stretch all the way back to the 1990s. Each time, they get less bang for the same buck. (That's exactly the playbook our central bank is using today.)

Right now, Japan stands on the precipice of its own new crisis, ignored as the euro debacle takes center stage. In order to avoid slipping into recession, Japan keeps on stimulating. In 2009 it doled out $100 billion. Added another $60 billion in 2010. Then it was struck with a magnitude 9 earthquake and put $48 billion into emergency funding.

But if you look at debt-to-GDP ratios, Japan is far and away the worst global player. Most countries get antsy when the debt-to-GDP crosses the 90 percent threshold. Japan's burgeoned to 200 percent. It has more public debt than any other place on the globe. The United States, however, is less than $400 billion behind.

Debt loading is something of a public service. The Bank of Tokyo Mitsubishi owns up to the fact that it has more government debt on its books than it does private loans or corporate bonds. Can you really call it a private enterprise? It's surely made a pact with Japan's feds.

Amazingly, Japan's borrowing costs are closer to Switzerland's for now. But we wager that this will be a point of contention once the weaker currency hands are flushed out of the global game.

What worries us most, is that Japan achieved its stagnant economy by funneling money into business investment and production-based infrastructure. But U.S. deficit spending goes mostly into consumer spending— the cornerstone of our GDP—and not investment. Where Japan flattened, so we'll plummet, unless we crib notes from another nation to our north.

The Wisdom of "Dr. No"

You know things are bad when the *Wall Street Journal* calls you "an honorary member of the Third World."

Why would they say that? Just another bond auction to fund the deficit right? Wrong. Financial officials were frantic, not a single bid came through until the final 30 minutes. That could be us any day now, but back in 1994, that was Canada's biggest problem.

Of the G7 countries, only Italy was worse off. The world dubbed Canada's dollar the "Northern peso."

~

We used to thank God that Italy was there because we were the second worst in the G7.

—*Scott Clark, associate deputy finance minister in the 1990s*

There was only one way to turn the fiscal ship around. Prime Minister Jean Chretien took an ax to social programs. The only bigger reduction in spending in Canada's history was the demobilization after World War II.

Of course, the magnitude wasn't as bad as what we're dealing with today. Back then, the world still had standards. Canada's 68 percent of debt to GDP in 1995/96 looks small compared to Italy's present 120 percent and Greece's whopping 140 percent.

The political tipping point came when the S&P dealt the Canadians a debt downgrade. Without the nice AAA rating, they were on ever shakier international ground (sound familiar?). Canada's costs to borrow money would get higher and higher.

Chretien took a big gamble after looking at the books. He was willing to risk holding his seat for only one term, if he could just solve the debt problem. He cared less about his career and more about being remembered for fixing this fiscal mess. His cabinet members also expected to be out of a job in short order when they heard his plan.

His first budget, released after just three months in office, cut defense spending, slashed foreign aid, closed tax loopholes, and ended a capital gains exemption. Then, after the near-failure of the bond auction, he called for a full-on spending freeze.

This was the man who as finance minister earned the moniker Dr. No! When asked at a ministry meeting for more money by one minister after he'd already turned down another, he said to his cabinet: "the next minister to ask for new money will see his whole budget cut by 20 percent." For every seven spending cuts, he raised one tax.

Was it painful? Yes. Cuts went as deep as 65 percent. Did it decimate whole government departments? Yes. Did it work? Yes.

By 1997, Chretien and his trusty finance minister, Paul Martin, had shrunk the deficit out of existence. Thus began the payoff decade. Canada outperformed the United States and trounced the other G7 nations when it came to growth, domestic investment, and best of all, job creation. It took the 2008 crisis to throw Canada's budget out of balance for the first time since their day. But its recession clouds haven't hung around like ours. Canada got back all the jobs lost already. But we've hardly made a dent.

So there's no truth to the idea we hear every election cycle: "spending promises are the only way to win elections." Prime Minister Chretien went on to enjoy two more terms! Frugality is actually still a political virtue. Well, at least if you live in Canada.

Now, what about the currency? The loonie traded at C$1.38 in 1995. It did weaken during the budget cutting, but now reaps the reward. The loonie achieved parity and still flirts within a few cents of that range. But politics and policy aren't the only things that help Canada's dollar, big oil revenues matter a lot here, as oil is Canada's biggest export.

We'll talk more about how to play Canada's strengths in "Currency Winners," but let me tell you why Canada's story is more important to us now than ever before.

The United States Reaches the 100 Percent Milestone

This isn't the kind of club you brag about joining. America has just become the newest member of the triple-digit debt-to-GDP club. Our current GDP stands at $15.18 trillion. Our debt burden now tops $15.4 trillion. Who else is a member? Well, Greece of course. Spain too. Portugal, Poland, Austria, Belgium, and France all shoulder heavy debts. On the spectrum, Japan shoots off the charts at over 210 percent.

Now here's what makes the U.S. situation even closer to Canada circa 1994. On August 5, 2011, the S&P stripped us of our AAA credit rating. Was that any kind of wake up call to Washington?

History shows that the people who save and invest grow and prosper, and the others deteriorate and collapse.

—Jim Rogers

Back in 2007, we saw the credit market drop to $3 trillion and wrote readers "maybe the rest of the world is sick and tired of our addiction to cheap credit."

Obviously we spoke too soon.

I ended 2011 down in Nicaragua with my fellow Agora Financial editor Chris Mayer. I shocked him and a dear reader one night when I said, "I'm long Treasuries, at least for the short term." They were beyond belief, but I think I am right.

Sure enough, a few weeks later, *BusinessWeek* boasts that the U.S. government received record demand for its bonds in 2011. Thus, they conclude glibly: "Barack Obama may have little difficulty financing a fourth consecutive year of $1 trillion budget deficits."

In the year that we were stripped of our perfect credit rating, our Treasuries returned investors in 10-year bills 25 percent.

Fact is, like the great Yogi Bera said: "It ain't over till it's over."

But keep in mind that the yield on these 10-year Treasuries has been in straight decline since 1981. You get paid zero interest to hold these securities. That's thanks to the Fed's Japan-inspired zero-rate policy. And like Japan, it seems we've not exhausted our debt tolerance yet. Amazing but true.

Marketeers are so jittery right now about what's going down in Europe that they wouldn't be caught dead holding Spanish bonds, so they throw them into the relative safety of the U.S. Treasury. Others like Boomers about to retire shy away from stocks (after what happened to them in dot-com dust-up). We're treated as the safe haven in a world of shrinking risk-free assets.

But how long does this really make sense without getting paid interest? Often, if you comb through the auction details with fine teeth, you'll find that in some auctions, only the "primary dealers" place bids. Turns out that these 21 primary dealers are required to bid. That's the only way they maintain their privilege. If such dealers weren't forced to bid, some of these deals would be left on the table.

So the world seems to say—for now—it's okay for Uncle Sam to borrow 42 cents for every dollar it spends. But if you do that, you'll have Citibank banging down your door to seize your house. You'd probably be considering filing for bankruptcy.

What's worse is that we're not alone when we issue our U.S. debt and play our Treasury tricks. We drag a whole bunch of nations along with us. In the next chapter let's explore the sick codependents: countries yoked to a dying currency.

Chapter Eight

Dollar Codependents

The Casino Game

WE'D LOVE TO SAY protecting yourself right now is as simple as cashing out of U.S. dollars. But that's not going to cut it. Things are far from simple. Just take the euro. You certainly wouldn't feel too confident putting your life savings in something whose dissolution is called for in daily headlines, but you would probably consider taking a European vacation sometime soon.

And, sure, maybe when you read this, the dollar may actually be strengthening against several global currencies.

That's why our publisher suggested we use "fluctuating"—not "shrinking" in our title. But we know you're smarter than that, and will be looking long term to see the kinds of scenarios that can play out.

As it happens, since all currencies draw their worth from nothing but the government's good word, something pretty dastardly could lie in store for more countries than just the United States. We're already seeing it unfold in the massive rashes of inflation around the globe.

But how did we get here?

Why *Is* the Dollar the World's Favorite?

The Fed is basically the credit card that the Treasury uses to finance the government's budget deficit.

Now hear this, foreign central banks do the same thing! And it's not because they love the United States or they want to help finance its borrowings. It's because they want to spend, spend, spend themselves.

Bank regulators from the domestic all the way to the big macro Basel authorities consider U.S. bonds as such high quality assets that you don't need bank reserves to back them up. So when foreign governments want to spend, they'll make good their overleveraged balance sheets by filling up on U.S. Treasuries. That's exactly why only 10 to 20 percent of the U.S. Treasury's debt is held by the private (read: nonbank, nongovernment) market.

The catch, as it was in the 2008 crisis, is to get on firm ground before the music stops. When newly created money flows through the banking system, you want to be the person who gets to it first, not last. And nobody wants to reveal the true cost of this money. They want to tell you it's free.

In 2002, when Ben Bernanke was a lowly new Fed hire addressing D.C.'s National Economists Club, he said just this:

> Under a fiat [that is, paper] money system, a government [in practice, the central bank in cooperation with other agencies] should always be able to generate increased nominal spending and inflation, even when the short term nominal interest rate is at zero.... The U.S. government has a technology, called a printing press (or, today, its electronic equivalent), that allows it to produce as many U.S. dollars as it wishes at essentially no cost.

But now there's a sign that some people are ready to get out of the party. Foreign central banks are cutting their holdings. And they're not stepping up to buy more at the auctions. Sure, other smaller investors have been taking their place. For now. We'll need more time to see if this is a new trend, but I'd keep your eye on it.

Only one thing kept the second half of 2011 from cementing a weakening demand curve for U.S. Treasuries into place. Japan started buying up U.S. dollars (debt-fueled all the way) to try and keep the yen weak against the dollar. The only place they could reasonably stash that dough was back into U.S. Treasuries.

I hope you're starting to see how currency and treasury markets are a rigged casino game. The rules and regs are written such that you can't choose where to put your money. Governments are choosing for you.

And while casinos are popular places, you'd hardly call them the soundest way to produce hard, cold wealth for generations.

Now here's where things get even trickier. In order to find the soundest currencies to change your money into, you might want to try choosing countries that participate in the fewest games. This soundly writes off the euro for all but short-term transactions. But you'll find there are some other surprises, even from traditional safe havens.

Plus, other opportunities arise from the relationships that two currencies have to one another, especially if you think that special relationship is going to change.

Now if you're wondering what I mean by *relationship*, I'll tell you right now, it's pegged. You saw pegging at work in Chapter 1 when you saw how gold was the measuring rod of value for the U.S. dollar, and all other currencies' values were fixed in relationship to the dollar. The legacy of that post-war move still hangs around today. But this 40-year hangover of floating, fixed, and pegged exchange rates might not last much longer.

Sometimes pegging gives a country and its currency some much-needed relief, but just like marriage that relationship can sour and prove a source of struggle, turmoil, and much unhappiness.

Why Peg?

In times of distress, a nation in currency trouble, battling a government bureaucracy mired in debt, will hoist the white flag of surrender and ask for a bunch of things. Usually one of them is IMF aid.

But how do you restore a currency's value when nothing stands under it, when everyone who holds it can't spend it fast enough, when investors the world over don't want to come into your country or put any investment into it, you have to get something to back you up. Or you need a bigger, richer government that is willing to foot the bill.

The easiest way to handle that is to choose a currency that does have solid value; that is, one that consumers and investors do believe in. (Often that currency is the one that runs the black market.)

In the ideal case, pegging a troubled currency will do good things. It'll limit the expansion of the country's money supply. That happens because the actions of a better central bank now determine policy. It's a way to break the chain of power.

Let's look at a few famous examples. (Keep in mind, though, these aren't stories that end in "happily ever after.")

Argentina 1991

Things here started to go downhill circa 1975. The end of military government left Argentina in a shambles by 1983. Unemployment was high, so was debt. The Falklands War didn't help. To fix things, they introduced a new currency—the austral—and made new loans. When Argentina couldn't pay even the interest on its debt, confidence in the austral collapsed. By 1989, the inflation rate topped 4,923 percent for the year.

After a period of raging hyperinflation, mass supermarket rioting, price controls, and other chaos, something had to be done.

On April 1, 1991, Argentina's Congress restored confidence. It put a currency board in place, guaranteeing a one-to-one peg with the dollar. And they only printed the amount of pesos they needed to get dollars on the foreign exchange market. So each peso in circulation was backed by a U.S. dollar. Dollar prices didn't change as quickly.

At the time, the strategy worked. (But as we'll see later, such boons don't last for long.)

Tequila Crisis 1994

In Mexico they call it "el error de diciembre"—or "the December Mistake." That's when the new president of Mexico abandoned tight currency controls. It was the classic cycle: Election year stimulus—which can't be paid for—leads to post-election blues.

Mexico didn't have the foreign exchange reserves it needed to preserve the value of its currency. So it had to devalue. Investors took one look and ran. They wouldn't buy the debt the government hoped to sell. Default loomed. The paralyzed banking system couldn't add confidence. The government couldn't keep the peso steady on their own. They allowed it to float.

Then–U.S. President Clinton stepped up with a line of credit for Mexico to buy pesos and give its currency some backbone. The United States backstopped Mexico's loans to keep it from defaulting.

So it should come as no surprise that Mexico's four largest banks, and 77 percent of all bank assets, are in foreign hands. The government is still paying bonds it used to buy bad debt from banks as a cure for the crisis. It took about a decade for credit to get back to "normal"—just in time for the next global crisis.

Asian Banking Crisis 1998

First there was the Asian economic miracle. Then came the crash.

In 1997, Asian central banks couldn't help themselves anymore. They held large current account deficits. They were addicted to foreign hot money flows.

Thailand, the epicenter, couldn't tackle the aftermath of a real estate bubble collapse. Thai stocks dropped 75 percent. Things began spiraling out of control when the government cut its peg to the U.S. dollar (the major component in a basket of currencies) and allowed the baht to float. It lost half of its value. The crisis ripped through Southeast Asia, devaluing stocks and destroying currency values. South Korea, Thailand, and Indonesia sent the SOS to the IMF to stabilize their currencies.

After Thailand, Malaysia was one of the nations to suffer the most. Before July 1997, Malaysia was a top investing destination, on the track to hit developed status by 2020.

Once currency speculators finished raiding the baht, they attacked the Malaysian ringgit. In despair, the premier clapped capital controls on the nation and pegged the ringgit to the U.S. dollar for seven years.

By 2005, Malaysia was a very different place. Bad banks were bought out by the stronger, better ones. Companies who couldn't get their financial house in order were delisted. Its current account deficit turned into a huge U.S. $14 billion surplus.

Today, the ringgit's not officially pegged to the dollar, but its currency board monitors its value against an undisclosed basket of currencies made up of trading partners and competitors.

Zimbabwe Hyperinflation circa 2006–2010

Zimbabwe used to be one of Africa's wealthiest and safest countries. But the meddlers and world-improvers helped put Mugabe in power. Since then, the place has gone to hell.

Having a civil war never helps anyone. In the case of Zimbabwe, food crisis joined with over 80 percent unemployment, flushing the economy into the toilet and destroying the lives of Zimbabweans.

In 2007, the government declared raising prices an offense worthy of arrest. But you simply can't outlaw inflation.

Things got so bad that the government stopped filing official statistics. At last count in July 2008, the inflation rate hit 231,150,889 percent. Yep, that's 231 million percent! By November 2008, Zimbabwe's inflation rate (as calculated by the Cato Institute) topped 516 quintillion percent. Only one hyperinflation in history has been worse: Hungary, 1946. (In Hungary, prices doubled every 15 hours.)

Over a third of the population left Zimbabwe. The black market reigned.

In early 2009, the central bank was printing new Zimbabwean dollars with 12 zeros lopped off the end. But no one wanted to touch them. So the finance minister threw up his hands. He sanctioned the use of other currencies: the U.S. dollar, the euro, the South African rand, and the Botswana pula.

"Inflation is coming back in style," our friend and mentor Bill Bonner wrote in *The Daily Reckoning* when Zimbabwe's top central banker, Gideon Gono was printing all those Zimbabwean dollars. "While other central bankers flounder, he's proven that you can have inflation . . . and have it more abundantly than you want.

Gono, if you haven't heard of him, is Robert Mugabe's right hand man. Gideon Gono, 47 years old, lives in a 47-bedroom mansion in Harare. He says he doesn't drink, only sleeps four hours a night, and runs regularly. He is known as "Mr. Inflation" for his Olympian efforts to increase the country's money supply. He does this the old-fashioned way—by printing pieces of paper with lots of-zeros on them. *Newsweek* seems to have found him in a talkative mood.

Asked what he thought of the worldwide credit crash, Gono replied:

> I sit back and see the world today crying over the recent credit crunch, becoming hysterical about something which has not even lasted for a year, and I have been living with it for 10 years. My country has had to go for the past decade without credit. . . . Out of the necessity to exist, to ensure my people survive, I had to find myself printing money. I found myself doing extraordinary things that aren't in the textbooks. Then the IMF asked the United States to please print money. I began to see the whole world now in a mode of practicing what they have been saying I should not.

So basically he's saying he's demonized for doing something that the West has done before, and will do again. It's the central bankers' main modus operandi the world over.

Right now, Zimbabweans await a new currency. Until then, they're using the U.S. dollar.

But troubled countries aren't the only nations with currencies yoked to our fate. There's still a pretty big list of nations who care what we're doing with our dollar.

The second big reason you peg is ease of trade. Why else do you think a country like Saudi Arabia lets

Washington decide its monetary policy? It's not because they agree with or really even like how we run things.

It has to do with oil. We want it, lots of it, and we are also at present the reigning reserve currency. To keep our currencies in line with the transactions we make buying and selling the raw crude and refined oil between us, we're pegged.

Not only is it convenient, it's practically by force! Back in 1973, when all monetary hell broke loose, Nixon made a secret deal with the Saudis to keep them using greenbacks only. In exchange for "protecting the oil fields" and giving weapons, the Saudis had to agree to use *only* U.S. dollars *and* to buy U.S. Treasuries with their oil profits. The resulting petrodollar is still with us today.

But Saudi Arabia isn't the only one. Most of the Arab world hitches itself to our cart horse. Qatar, Oman, the United Arab Emirates, Bahrain, Jordan all make the list.

The Hong Kong dollar is pegged, and China's yuan is pegged to the U.S. dollar with just a hint of float. Sure, there are some good things from all this. Hong Kong made it through the Asian financial crisis that endangered its neighbors. It survived a raid by the famed speculator George Soros. And, in July 1997, it sailed through the Brits' handoff of the island to China, ending 156 years of colonial rule. So perhaps that was the smartest move Hong Kong could make in 1983. But there's change afoot.

Right now, Hong Kong is debating whether to abandon its 27-year peg to the U.S. dollar, because, as you'll see below, there's a dark side to pegging.

Why Not to Peg?

The nation that tethers its currency to another's is not free.

To keep your currency in line with the peg, you have to resort to all sorts of currency intervention to preserve the relationship. Just as we saw Japan doing in 2011 (though its relationship to the dollar is not as formal as some).

If you, as a nation, act like Japan, then you get stuck with massive currency reserves to keep your own currency, in this case the yen, from appreciating. That's a lot of work, and that's only the beginning of your trouble.

Say the country you're pegged to has bad monetary policy. You can't put a stop to it. You don't have a voice in what they're doing. In fact, what usually happens is that you follow suit.

Today, Hong Kong is a perfect example of this peril. It is stuck between two monetary regimes, the United States and China. It's got two masters, and it would rather be free. By maintaining its peg, Hong Kong is stuck "importing" two things: inflation and raging property prices.

Hong Kong can't say no to the lousy U.S. interest rate policy, no matter what's going on locally. In this case, the United States slumps and demands near-zero rates like a defibrillator on a dead man, while Hong Kong is booming, bolstered by the growth in mainland China. So property prices are up 70 percent since 2009. Inflation climbs at its fastest pace since 1995.

For Hong Kong, 1995 wasn't a good year. The same devil—ultra-low interest rates—brought it to the brink. The rates pushed up property prices to record highs by 1994, only to see everything tumble the next year. It's a crisis they'd love to avoid today.

If Hong Kong were in control of its own monetary policy, it could tackle inflation on its own. Now here's the thing. Any change could increase instability in the short term, so chances are, the peg won't be ditched any time soon. After all, what currency is better? Even a basket of currencies wouldn't necessarily do the trick. Nothing looks good right now, not the pound, not the euro, not even the safety of the Swiss franc.

Pegging Destroyed This Safe Haven

You know the old hope—that one day some distant relative will pass on and leave you their entire fortune: a secret Swiss savings account. There's some reason to it.

The Swiss franc was, until just last year, in the running for one of the strongest, solid currencies in the world for not decades, but centuries!

However, in September 2011, the Swiss National Bank put the kibosh on the party. It staged the biggest franc intervention since the 1970s. The Swiss franc is now pegged to the fate of the euro.

That means plenty for savvy investors, and they knew it. On the day of the announcement, the franc fell off a cliff, dropping 10 percent in an instant. Likewise, gold priced in Swiss francs vaulted to 1620 per troy ounce, from 1497 in less than 60 seconds.

For some, this signals the alarm that precious metals—gold, silver, platinum—are the only safe havens left, now that the Swiss have surrendered sovereignty over their economic fate.

The Swiss central bank pledged to defend its minimum exchange rate of 1.20 francs versus the euro. The means? Unlimited currency purchases. Plus, it'll keep the benchmark rate at zero.

Policy will now be decided by the EU and for the EU (or rather for the benefit of some EU members, at the expense of others), and the Swiss will have to go along for the ride. We suspect it'll be like the rapids ride at your local amusement park. Everyone takes a bath, but the first are laughed at the most.

But what was Switzerland to do? Its currency, like the U.S. dollar, suffers from the same popularity problem. Switzerland says its exports were suffering at the hands of a too-strong currency, as more and more dollars, yen, reals, and what have you flooded into Swiss currency.

So now, we're faced with this reality: The Swiss want you to keep your money!

Watch Out for This Government Crackdown

We're not saying this will happen tomorrow, but when the government sees citizens are unhappy and are willing to move their money in ever greater numbers and amounts, they'll shut you out of important money moves. It's best if you get a jump on them!

Right now, we're watching for the signs like a hawk. We're seeing it happen already, again, in Argentina.

First, they re-elect their populist president by a landslide during a time of high inflation. Her idea of reigning in state spending and high inflation is subsidy cuts and "fine-tuning" her nation's demand-driven model. Argentina will not import "a single nail," she vows.

So now Argentines will have trouble getting things like good Italian pasta, as all importers will have to get permission to bring goods into the country via the tax authorities. If it's something Argentines make, then no dice for the importer.

Or you have to agree to an arrangement. If you import cars, for example, expect to export soya or wine to compensate, dollar-for-dollar. That's great, except when you have a bad harvest. Then what do you do?

Well, never fear, wage and price controls are on the way. And the Central Bank of Argentina is ready to plan another big increase of the money supply this year; upping the cash flowing into the market by over 26 percent. (So we shouldn't be surprised that Argentine inflation estimates top 24 percent.) Capital has been flying from Argentine states at the rate of $3 billion per month.

But the politicians aren't listening. Why try to cool the economy by something smart, like interest rates? It's far easier to print, print, print! (Plus, who isn't printing right now?)

All this lays the groundwork for something more sinister. On October 31, 2011, Argentina imposed currency controls—to limit access to U.S. dollars. There, the U.S. dollar is still considered valuable property. So valuable that Argentines withdrew $654 million in dollar-denominated deposits from private-sector banks during the first week of November. That's a 4.3 percent drop in total dollar deposits in just five days.

Argentine citizens reacted by securing as many dollars as they could—while they still had the chance.

The government's excuse? To crack down on money laundering.

But, according to the Dow Jones News Service, "Most analysts say the real aim of the crackdown on dollar purchases is to stem capital flight that has cut central bank reserves to $46.57 billion from $52 billion in early August."

In other words, people want to dump increasingly worthless pesos.

What does that look like on the street level? We turn to our man on the scene, *Daily Reckoning's* Joel Bowman for comment: "The official exchange rate is 4.28 pesos for every one U.S. dollar. But on the black market—or the 'blue market,' as it's known here—the rate is as high as 5.2-to-1."

The large gap between the two extremes is because there's a shortage of dollar sellers.

This currency clamp-down isn't new to Argentines. They're getting awfully used to it. By 1998, its currency peg caused more hurt than help. The year 2001 ended with a run on banks. The president said Argentine debt no longer had the guarantee that it'd be paid. More rioting. The president resigned. Soon after, the interim president resigned.

Then in 2002, drastic currency controls locked down Argentines' money. Imagine if the U.S. government were to do this:

- Limit withdrawals to $1,000 (1,500 pesos) per month.
- Freeze checking accounts over $10,000 and turning them into 1-year CDs.
- Freeze saving accounts over $3,000 and turning them into 1-year CDs.
- Converting smaller accounts into peso-denominated holdings at a fixed exchange rate.

It happened in Argentina then. It could happen to them again today. It could happen to us tomorrow.

We've long thought that currency controls are just a matter of time. With the mounting national debt, something's gotta give. The easy something is always the nation's money. But have you thought about what you'll do when that day arrives?

For some farseeing Americans the prospect of becoming trapped by their government in a worthless currency is not a historical curiosity: It's a matter of urgent action.

Already there are virtual Berlin Walls shooting up around Americans and their money, but these Argentinean developments remind us that it can happen at a moment's notice.

You're not helpless, and the currency research in the next chapter can give you solutions to put in place today . . . just in case.

Things to Watch for . . .

- Arab nations break their dollar currency pegs. They could adopt the "Khaleeji"—consider it a Gulf states "euro"—as soon as 2015.
- France has already lost its AAA rating. Look for other European nations—even Germany—to lose the same.
- Greece pulls out of the euro.
- Japanese and U.S. cost of borrowing starts to climb.
- Fewer bidders show up at Treasury auctions.
- European bail out mechanism gets overloaded.
- United States steps in to help euro bailout further.
- China or Hong Kong break dollar pegs.

Chapter Nine

The Dollar's Days Are Numbered

~

What the Gold Market Tells Me . . .

MANY OF THE MARKET experts we interviewed for this book might think the dollar has a way to go yet, but whether they think it's five years or several decades, they *all* say that the gold market has spoken! They believe the gold market tells us that the dollar's days are numbered.

Why do they think that? Just look at what the gold market's been up to in the past decade—as our central bankers and world leaders took control of the economy.

Here's where gold closed on the final day of each year since 2000:

2000: $273.60

2001: $279.00

2002: $348.20

2003: $416.10

2004: $438.40

2005: $518.90

2006: $638.00

2007: $838.00

2008: $889.00

2009: $1,096.50

2010: $1,421.40

2011: $1,566.80

It's gone up every single year since the dot-com bubble burst. The big milestones: Gold first jumped above $1,000 an ounce on March 13, 2008. It reached a new record high on September 6, 2010 of $1,923.70.

Lest you think that the run is over, keep in mind that, if we adjust for inflation, we're still well below the old 1980s high, which would be over $2,200.

As newsletter legend and octogenarian Richard Russell says: "To my knowledge, this is the longest bull market of any kind in history in which each year's close was above the previous year. This fabulous bull market will not end with a whisper and a fizzle. I continue to believe that the upside gold crescendo of this bull market lies ahead."

Richard expects the wake-up call for the average investor to be when the Dow breaks below 10,000.

We suggest you not wait to act.

———————————— ≈ ————————————

We believe the market has already made gold the new reserve currency. The governments and central banks haven't officially adopted it yet, but the market has voted gold in by revaluing it upwards for the past 10 years against all paper currencies.

—*Eric Sprott, Sprott Asset Management*

Most of the smart money is in gold. Consider a few of the guys who've called some big crises in the past.

George Soros dumped most of his gold holdings in 2011—but now he's back in. He's holding shares of

SPDR Gold Trust (GLD). GLD is the biggest exchange traded fund (ETF) that's backed by gold.

John Paulson won fame for calling the housing bubble, and cashing out on a $15 billion bet against housing. Paulson plunged into GLD in 2009.

He was the largest shareholder in GLD, and in June 2011 he pared down his holdings from 21 million shares to 20.3 million. (We expect it was mostly to take those profits to pay off those who couldn't forgive him for making a play on Citigroup and the Chinese fraud Sino-forest.)

What other gold stocks is he holding? Paulson & Co holds shares in the third-largest gold producer: AngloGold Ashanti Ltd. It's the largest holder. Paulson & Co also holds shares in stocks like Gold Fields, NovaGold Resources Inc., Randgold Resources, Agnico-Eagle, Barrick Gold, and International Tower Hill Mines. He also agrees with us on the good prospects of Iamgold Corp.—one we've followed closely over the years.

Meanwhile, I think it's worth checking out what the big buyers of gold are up to. Not all central bankers have bonehead policies; in fact, several countries' banks are taking any correction they see as a chance to back up the truck and take on another load of solid asset treasure.

SOLUTION!

Hold Gold How You Like It

The GLD was introduced in November 2004, prices have more than tripled since. People like it because it's an extremely liquid way to get upside to gold. Conspiracies abound as to how much backing these new ETFs really have. If you're concerned, we say the best gold is what you have stored safely under lock and key, whether in a foreign bank or in a safe bolted to your basement floor. If it has a unique serial number on it, you'll know it's yours.

"Biggest Central Bank Gold Rush in 40 Years?"

That's a recent headline screaming out from the front page of the *Financial Times*. Central banks, you see, were buying up during the September correction, putting them on track to buy more gold in 2011 than at any time since Bretton Woods fell apart 40 years ago. The World Gold Council predicted around 450 tons would change hands.

Who's buying the most? Russia snapped up 15 tons in 2011. Thailand bought 20 tons. Bolivia added 15 tons to its stash. Kazakhstan and Tajikistan also added to their gold piles. It marks the first time in a generation that central bank gold holdings expanded. Emerging markets, you see, really want to catch up and hold at least 2 to 8 percent of their reserves in gold.

Really, as strategist and CNBC regular Michael Pento put it, the only "enemies" of gold are "rising interest rates and a balanced budget." And these are things we won't be seeing in the West anytime soon. Smaller central banks have every reason to hedge up happily on gold.

Who might really step up purchases at every correction? China may invest more than $1 trillion in bullion, Pento says, "China wants to be an international player, and they need to own more gold than they currently have."

As of six months ago, China held only 1.8 percent of its total reserves in gold, Russia 8.7 percent, and India 9.5 percent. They have a lot of catching up to do. And they're ready, willing, and able to do it.

In the United States, the figure is 76.5 percent, assuming that all the gold last audited in Fort Knox in the 1950s is still there. All 147.3 million ounces. Cross your fingers.

We consider this tantamount to a realization that gold is king and fiat currencies have nowhere to go but down. The central banks may deny it at press conferences, but they know better in the privacy of their own gold transactions. The gold is what they depend on to hedge any currency losses.

Not only are central banks in these nations ready to gobble gold, the citizens are very hip to gold acquisition. Although we must admit, many of them have been so for centuries.

Let's first check out the place where it's a wedding tradition.

Gold Buyers 'R' Us

Asia's third-largest economy is the world's largest consumer of precious metal. India loves gold. They own nearly $1 trillion of the stuff. That's equivalent to half of India's nominal GDP (in dollar terms).

And as the rupee weakens, you can bet they'll keep buying. Peak time is between October through January—the wedding season. But this is a bigger story than glamorous nuptial necklaces. They're importing so much gold that they're in danger of growing their current account deficit beyond the breaking point. That's because they import 92 percent of what they buy.

At present 8 percent of Indians' savings is locked into gold, which is usually passed on for generations.

Perhaps the biggest citizen's case of safe haven Asian buyers is Vietnam.

My man on the scene, "Capital & Crisis" editor Chris Mayer, got the scoop while staying in the Sofitel Metropole, one of the world's great hotels, while wrapping up his own book, *World Right Side Up*.

"Among all the teak wood and ceiling fans and posh service," he writes, "you can drift back and imagine the golden age of travel." You can even take that nostalgia for a drive (if you have the cash), as a pair of classic 1956 Citroëns stand out front ready to deliver.

That's the surface of the situation, anyways. By the poolside bar, Chris met with a contact in Hanoi. "Welcome to Vietnam," he said. "Your timing is no good."

The contact (whose name is withheld at his request) is close to the prime minister and others of political power in Vietnam. He didn't say anything too controversial, at least nothing that raises an eyebrow in the States right now.

He said, "Vietnam is in a very dangerous situation." He cited huge budget deficits and high inflation. Officially, the Vietnamese inflation rate is 20 percent. "And I am not sure," he confessed, "that the prime minister has the willingness to fight this inflation. Vietnam will probably suffer a lot."

As you can guess, the Vietnamese central bank repeatedly devalued the dong in relation to the U.S. dollar and other major currencies—thanks to overissuance. (Sound like a familiar pattern?)

The Vietnamese buy more gold per capita than anyone else in the world. They even pay 9 to 11 percent premiums over the world gold price to get it.

This flight from the dong doesn't please the government. One way to discourage gold ownership is to cut the number of gold bar producers in the country—turning it into a monopoly. One sole producer, SJC, will control 90 percent of the market.

Expect then a huge black market in gold products. Already there's a huge black market demand for U.S. dollars, anything to get out of increasingly worthless dong.

Chris concludes, and it seems the Vietnamese agree, "The Vietnamese dong is truly an awful currency." It takes about 21,000 dong to get one dollar. In 2008, it was about 16,000. Consider that's falling in relation to a currency we wouldn't consider a pillar of strength.

It also means that if you're angling for gains in Vietnamese stocks, you have to outpace monetary depreciation before you even begin to make some real money. So you see why the Vietnamese are clamoring to buy gold . . . and why the government would rather they not sock away wealth into this hard asset over investing in the broader economy.

Just how toxic is the dong? Back to Chris:

> On my way home, I went through Bangkok again. I forgot to change all my dong before I left Vietnam. So I went to the money-changers in Bangkok to convert my dong to dollars. The Thai money-changers would have nothing to do with the dong. It made me think well of the Thais. So I wound up bringing home some

colorful currency with Uncle Ho's portrait as souvenirs.

Chris points to the Mekong Exploration Commission (1866–1868). The French explorer Francis Garnier led a group to the Mekong River region. What they brought with them again points to gold as a timeless, borderless store of value.

These Frenchmen didn't use francs. They brought Mexican silver dollars, gold bars, and Siamese silver ticals. Gold—and sister silver—are truly universal when it comes to monetary appeal. Forget fumbling over exchange rates. A gold bar is a currency everyone can understand.

Gold Is Getting Harder to Find

The increasing demand makes gold harder to find. We're not talking about deposits in mines here. We're saying that if you want anything more than a little bit of bullion you'll find a lot less on the market.

"People are coming directly to us" for large gold purchases, says the CEO of one of the world's biggest gold miners.

"They're finding it's very difficult to secure the volume of gold they want," says Mark Cutifani of AngloGold Ashanti, in an interview with the website

Bull Market Thinking. He describes these customers as "people who want tonnes of physical gold, people with serious financial muscle.

"That's something we've noticed over the last 18 months, and it's been increasing in the last six months. I think people are finding it's hard to get physical gold" via other channels.

And if you visit the local coin shop on a week when the gold price slips from a peak, don't expect you'll be able to get a bargain that you can take home in your pocket. Last time we went looking, we had to call a bunch of dealers and finally get one to sell us some from his private stash.

So you're probably wondering, if there's a de facto gold standard at work in the markets—and increasingly popular in the minds of your average citizen, why isn't there a national or international gold standard?

There used to be. And, we say, it's inevitable that there will be again.

No nation in history has ever survived fiat money, money that did not have a precious metal backing.

—*Ronald Reagan, 1980*

A Return to Sound Money

The best monetary system is the one that offers the most stability, day-to-day, year-to-year, century-to-century. Throughout history, we've seen that the gold standard is the standard of stability. Even when followed imperfectly, it's far better than a devaluation-based floating system. Haven't we seen that just since the end of World War II, monetary devaluations—the first route to solving a crisis—never create a lasting fix. Instead, devaluations set the stage for future strife.

A gold standard links the value of a paper dollar to the value of gold. This keeps the money supply in check, because there must be a means to adjust the supply of money so that the currency maintains its fixed value relative to gold.

A quarter is always a fixed value—25 cents—to the dollar, right? Why should the dollar be any different in regard to gold?

The discipline that gold-dollar convertibility imposes would fix a lot of problems we've written about in these pages.

It would clap handcuffs on Treasury's access to its Federal Reserve credit card. If the Federal Reserve created more money than individuals in the market wanted to hold, people would get rid of the inflationary excess by promptly exchanging paper dollars for the gold equivalent.

This in turn would force banks to be solvent, and have higher reserves. It would force Congress to no longer use the Treasury like an ATM card on promises it can't pay for.

Obviously, the dollar isn't worth 1/35 an ounce of gold as Franklin Roosevelt decreed at the twilight of our last gold standard. To set it at $1,000 per ounce is still a pretty radical devaluation of the dollar.

Every day, the market is deciding the de facto value of gold in relation to all the paper currencies in the world. Eventually, governments will have to take note of it too and accept it.

If you got a start in politics after 1971, you've only ever known the era of soft money operations where you spend your way into office and stay there for decades. Likewise, if you got your start in banking in, say, the heyday of the 1980s, you're addicted to the moves you can make on soft money. Remember the day when selling bonds was considered boring?

We're financial writers, our job is to write about the markets in exciting and useful ways, but we confess, we'd rather see the day where we shut our laptops and say there's simply nothing urgent to tell people to do today.

There's nothing we need to protect them from. Their bank accounts are paying good interest.

We fear that day won't come as soon as we hope, which is exactly why we're writing this.

It's why we suggest you get yourself a few bricks of gold (or a few junk bags of silver) if you do nothing else we've suggested in this book.

In case you're still not convinced, or you have a few doubts, read the next section carefully. Let's tackle a few myths about gold (and the gold standard).

Myth No. 1: We're Running Out of Gold

So we're not running out of gold. But perhaps one day, quips a blogger, we will run out of myths about the gold standard. The market makers and central bankers want you to think there's simply not enough gold around today to support a gold standard. They say there are too many complexities in the market for gold to back it. (Read "complexities" as too much easy money to be gained by the few who profit the most.)

We owe this bit of myth busting to George Mason economics professor, Larry White at a Cato Conference. The U.S. Treasury, he says, does own enough gold to back our dollar reserves—so long as they're not lying about what gold they've got. The U.S. government holds a total of 261.5 million ounces—147.3 million of those ounces are in Fort Knox. At a conservative $1,600 per ounce value for gold, we're looking at a $418.4 billion gold holding.

Now let's flip over the cocktail napkin. If we add up the sum of all currency and checking account balances (M1 in econ speak), we get $2.1 trillion. Divide 418.4 billion by 2.1 trillion, and we get a 19.9 percent reserve ratio. Historically speaking, that's quite healthy.

Current required bank reserves are only $83 billion. So the value of our gold is over five times what banks currently hold to back their reserves. That's like saying for every dollar we hold, we'd have 20 cents of gold backing it.

That's great coverage and far better than what's happening now. Even if you're conservative and use only the value of gold in Fort Knox, you'll get a reserve ratio of 11.2 percent. "Lower, but still healthy," says Professor White.

We admit that gold production is never a constant. Production in the famous South African mines has dropped off since the 1980s, while China has risen to become the world's largest gold producer. However, we've been exploring for gold since the New World was young, and a place where Christopher Columbus found no gold can actually become a producing region today with higher prices and new mining techniques.

New mines are springing up all the time in places like the Canadian Maritimes or even a little old mining town in South Carolina.

Myth No. 2: Gold Is Risky

This next bit of myth is busted by Agora Financial's main resource analyst, Byron King. He says simply: "Gold has been risky since I started buying it at $300 per ounce, back in 2001."

So sure, gold is risky, but there are far worse risks out there (like not buying yourself a little peace-of-mind insurance, making up about 10 percent of your portfolio at the very least.)

From its current level near $1,700 per ounce, gold could decline to, say, $1,500 or $1,300 or less.

Why would that happen? Think back to Paulson's case above. Sure he placed the right bet on gold, but he didn't on Citi. It tanked. Likewise, if there's a massive market crash, you will see a lot of gold selling—so folks have ready cash to meet margin calls.

Remember 2008? Gold sold down from about $1,000 to about $750. Still, that 25 percent haircut was mild, compared with what happened to the rest of the market. And through it all—the crash and turmoil—gold remained liquid. Somebody bought that gold. So gold is good, especially when people need fast cash.

Looking ahead, gold has a huge upside. The gold price could accelerate and levitate up to $2,500. Or maybe even $5,000.

As long as politicians everywhere spend more than their country can afford, this gold-investing stuff is kind of easy: Buy, hold, and wait.

Now here's the backing behind gold. Its fundamentals of supply and demand also suggest that its price will rise.

We've seen the gold souks of Dubai and the Cai Bai gold market in China. We've seen men with fat wads of currency, any currency, peeling off the bills to buy, buy, buy.

Meanwhile, global mine output is shrinking. The famous old big mines of South Africa are just too deep (three to four kilometers deep!) and too hard to keep running at the levels of their former glory. All it would take is even one major accident that could cause numerous mines to shut down, and then South African gold output would fall off a cliff.

Myth No. 3: Gold Is in a Bubble

Gold and gold stocks are just a tiny slice of the financial world's asset pie. You can take that in absolute terms or relative to how much gold they were holding in the past.

Back in 1921, gold made up 28 percent of global assets. In 1932, it was 20 percent. By 1948, it shot up to 30 percent. In 1981, as Volker was getting things back under control, 26 percent of global holdings were glittery gold.

Today? Gold is barely 1 percent of global assets. That's hardly the stuff of a bubble—all this price frenzy of the past few years is barely a blip on the radar screen.

Only when every CNBC TV special is on junior gold miners and half of your average target retirement fund is in gold exchange-traded funds (ETFs) will we say we're in high danger bubble territory for a crash.

Myth No. 4: We Can't Have a Gold Standard

Lewis Lehrman (Ron Paul's co-author on *The Case for Gold*) addressed this topic at the Heritage Foundation's Stable Dollar Conference.

He admitted that the gush of money from 2009–2011 went straight into the pockets of the banking class, with "apologies to his fellow bankers in the room." He admitted we have a "Rogue Fed."

The cure: gold standard. His prescription: Take a survey of the average cost of gold production round the world and the average cost of margin. That gets us a $1,000 base for gold, with a value up to $3,000 on the high end.

Nathan Lewis, author of *Gold: The Once and Future Money*, makes a clean, simple case for a return to the gold standard. As he put it, "We were on gold standard for 182 years, it's not that kooky." And he adds that no disaster caused us to go off. He's not alone. Even former NY Fed governor Lawrence Lindsay told the Heritage crowd we'll see specie money within the next 10 years.

Lindsay thinks the Fed should issue gold coins and let monetary choice do its work. Is he hopeful? Maybe not. He said: "Society is demanding too much! No one can pull this off!" Nice when a Fed governor knows his limits, too bad he's no longer on the FOMC. His final summation was: "We're all gonna be a little bit poorer ten years from now."

Judy Shelton, meanwhile, suggests this opening salvo: a Treasury-issued gold-backed bond. Russia did it under Putin. Is this risking the family jewels? Sure, she says, but this is a family emergency. Who should be in charge? Not the Fed. "These are people for whom stable inflation is not an oxymoron," she points out. That's exactly why you should be worried. Gold is the cure.

For the secret to the trick of making the gold standard work, we return to the fine work of Nathan Lewis. The idea of 100 percent gold backing is the biggest myth, and hence the biggest obstacle.

We've never really had 100 percent reserve gold backing, but we did have successful stability. From 1833 until just before the Civil War, we averaged 20 to 40 percent gold backing. Post-war, with our fiscal house back in order (1880–1900) we had a 25 percent average.

In short, you don't need all the gold in the world to enjoy a gold standard. From 1775 to 1900 the base money supply increased 163 times. Meanwhile gold in the world only grew 3.4 times in the same period.

The Brits left off the gold standard in 1797 and came back to it in 1821. "They just kind of did it, not a big deal," says Lewis. Here's how they make it work.

"Little gold, lotta brains" is how Lewis lauds the then-Bank of England. It averaged 1.5 percent of gold holdings in the world—a mere seven million ounces—yet remained on a gold standard.

Having gold backing on whatever you got, and delivering gold when you're asked for it, is all you need to do. Between the 1880s to 1914, the Old Lady of Threadneedle Street had a small horde: £20–£40 million. Meanwhile, France and Russia each kept closer to £100 million. Yet the Brits were the most trusted monetary brand on the planet and the world's reserve currency.

The foible comes during World War II, when the Yank central bank tries to take the crown. It's a lesson in how not to do it the next time around.

"Lots of gold, little brain" is how Lewis characterized U.S. banking brawn.

By the end of 1941 we had 44 percent of the world's gold in our coffers. The highest occupancy of gold bars ever at Fort Knox was in December—649.6 million ounces.

It was a brief 100 percent gold reserves period, but the system failed in a short 27 years. Our chronic problem was never contracting our money supply. Like ever.

In 1945, we were the tops. We rebuilt nations and set up debt obligations that lasted for decades. Meanwhile, we stopped worrying about whether we could deliver the goods in gold to anyone who wanted 'em in exchange for a dollar. That's exactly how we bungled our world reserve status at its very infancy.

It's amazing we've held on so long.

That said, we've asked a bunch of experts how they want to play the last stages of the end game. Some are more pessimistic than others.

When we asked Eric Sprott which currencies he'd prefer to the USD, he said, in a word, none. "They're all ugly in our opinion. There's no currency that stands out. In the race to the bottom, some will look better than others, but they're all on the same path. We prefer to hold physical precious metals."

Even though he swore to us he's not a dollar bear, John Mauldin admits this much: "I still buy gold every month regardless! And hope it goes down!" (as many do, so they can buy more).

In short, even though he sees the dollar rising against real losers like the euro and the pound, he does expect it to fall against some others. After 2014, he's not willing to comment. What matters is if—and that's a big if—the United States gets its fiscal house in order, starting with Congress. If they don't, says Mauldin, "the dollar takes a real dive."

With that in mind, let's prepare further, by exploring currency plays you could make in the near term, while you pad your asset holdings with gold over the long-haul.

Chapter Ten

Currency Winners

❧

Forward Thinking Moves from Smart Investors

IN OUR CAPACITY AS publisher of Agora Financial, a world-leader in financial advisories for individual investors, we meet a wide variety of interesting voices in the financial community. Some with whom we agree. Many of whom we don't. Here are a few of the more important former.

We asked one of our favorite resource investors, Rick Rule, what currency he would prefer to hold his portfolio in.

Rick Rule Bets on the Chilean Peso

Rick Rule gave us the goods, starting first and foremost with gold and silver bullion.

He admits to holding U.S. dollars (only because he lives part time in the United States). He likes New Zealand's strong dollar-high real interest rate policy, but don't jump on that just yet.

The catch is that he, like we, is a little circumspect about their current account and trade deficits relative to GDP.

But here's the currency he likes without reservation: the Chilean peso. He calls it "the best-run economy on the planet." Probably doesn't hurt that it is very mining friendly.

Rule also likes the Loonie (for the reasons we suspected in Chapter 7). And for the crowning finish, he's holding a small speculative position in Russian rubles.

Michael Covel Gives a Total Strategy

Michael Covel, founder of TurtleTrader.com, thinks the great opportunities in traditional investing are dead. Forget buy and hold, he says. In manipulated, manufactured markets, uncertainty rules and surprise is the order of the day.

This spells one certainty: volatility.

Regular crashes are the best-case scenario. Complete market collapse is the worst.

Does this have him discouraged? Far from it.
He told us:

> As I look ahead I can safely make one predic-
> tion: all markets will trend either up or down.
> Unfortunately, there is no way to know for
> sure when each market will rise or fall. Across
> this backdrop I consider technical trend fol-
> lowing strategies one of your best chances to
> profit and protect what you already have. If
> you look ahead 10 years into the future, and
> the USD has crashed by 50 percent, trend fol-
> lowing will be the one strategy that will have
> made the most money via a dollar collapse. It
> will ride the dollar down, euro down and gold
> up and make money on all three. And if there
> is a reversal, it will ride 'em back the other
> way. Trend following's agnostic nature makes
> it the single best investing opportunity today.

Chuck Butler Goes for the Renminbi

The Chinese renminbi, Chuck informs us, has gained
27 percent versus the dollar since it dropped its peg to
the dollar in July of 2005.

While 27 percent in almost seven years might not
sound like a great investment, it's a great start.

Chuck thinks that anyone who bought 7 years ago, got in on the ground floor of a currency that will—in the next 10 years—be backed by gold, and own the reserve currency of the world title. That's a stunning statement worth considering. For the next five years, at least, he anticipates the Chinese will only allow a gradual appreciation of the renminbi. So you still have a shot.

To this we'll add a list from Bill Bonner that puts the trajectory of China into perspective:

- Who's number one in steel production? China.
- Who's number one in mobile phones? Well, China again.
- Who's number one in manufacturing output? That would be China, too.
- How about car sales? China.
- How about exports? China.
- Patents granted? China.
- Energy consumption? China.
- Fixed investment? China.

In our minds, that does say a lot about China's rising influence on markets; we've been there, we've seen its empty malls, and we know it's got some big problems to tackle, but it's done plenty to get ahead. And they'll do what they can to stay there.

Jim Rogers's Home Currency: The Singapore Dollar

We didn't get to interview Jim for this book, but he agreed with the tenets of our book *Financial Reckoning Day Fallout*. We always keep an eye on what he's up to. He's made Singapore one of his main homes starting in 2007. We think that's a good clue as to what he feels about its local currency—the Singapore dollar. He's strongly for it and thinks it'll keep value promises.

Here's the evidence in its favor that we've dug up.

1. Here's a currency that models itself on former safe-haven Swiss franc.
2. Over the past decade the Singapore dollar strengthened against the USD by 37 percent.
3. Predictions say it'll hit parity by 2015.
4. The Monetary Authority of Singapore likes strength.
5. The economic forecasts suggest there's growth here that's not going away.

Peter Cooper Gives One to Avoid . . . and Three to Buy

Peter Cooper ventures that the British pound has the most value to lose over the next two years—even more than the dollar. It's a fat hen sitting on a secret pile of the highest debts of any major economy. For the moment, it's congratulating itself for staying out of the Eurozone, but they can't break out any bubbly yet.

He drew our attention to "Project Armageddon" done by brokers Tullett Prebon. They claim that the Brits have plenty more to worry about than their EU brothers; it's just that their debts won't come due until later.

The Brits owe a staggering £5 trillion ($8.3 trillion).

Included in this number are public pension liabilities, public-private partnerships, and £1.34 trillion in financial sector bailouts. Total public debt is 244 percent of GDP.

If you count external debt, the study points out, the UK has a higher debt-to-GDP than all the countries making headlines today. You know them: Greece, Portugal, and Spain.

UK skates by while the world is distracted, but it's only a matter of time before the market starts pricing the Brits' debt accordingly.

It doesn't matter whether Europe gets its act together or crashes. Either way, says Peter, the pound is vulnerable.

In a situation like we're in, where we'll all be racing to devalue and get back on track, the biggest loser will be the country with the highest total debt to GDP. And that's Britain.

UK worries are exactly the kind we face. They're still in housing bubble hangover after the single biggest debt binge: mortgage borrowing from 2002 to 2009. Housing had gone up about 70 percent, but the euphoria didn't last.

In order to keep its banking system alive, it'll resort to devaluation and inflation. But like the dollar, it shall fare okay at first, as the euro mess sorts itself out.

How long will Brits keep their super-low borrowing rate? Their beloved pound lost its place as the world's reserve currency after World War II bankrupted them. Its devaluation is a long, painful descent from global dominion. (Something we're likely to sympathize with in the years ahead.)

If you're looking for a safe place to stash your cash, we conclude that sterling isn't for you. We have every reason to agree with Peter Cooper. In fact, we'll take the truth from the mouth of a Brit. One of our dear pen pals recently described a visit from a Chinese government delegation of investors to his offices a stone's throw from Parliament.

We'd wondered what he was going to tell them, and how they would take it!

He writes that one or two of the Chinese visitors will always be hip to the sound-money theorists, but if you mention Marx in a good light, they'll still applaud. Beyond bizarre, but it probably helped them take to our friend's message (or at least he thinks his message took).

He writes:

> They are clearly suspicious about all those
> U.S. bonds and don't know what to make of
> them. I sense no great appetite to come to
> Europe's aid, either. Indeed, I told them to run
> a million miles from us.

When he launched into his discussion about the sheer
level of debt and the high-risk money printing stimulus
game, they were stunned.

> They all just stared in that sort of way an
> 18-year-old girl would if an older man suddenly
> plunged his hand unexpectedly up her skirt to
> fondle her bottom. No one moved or reacted.
> They all just sat there and stared frozen with,
> well, who knows what. . . .

Ah, you can always trust a Brit for some good gallows humor.

But back to our man in Arabia, Peter Cooper . . . for
some currencies he does like.

1. Dirham—he confesses that "being from the Arab
   Gulf states, we quite like the dollar-pegged dirham."

Lest you think that's nonsense, based on what you read in Chapter 8, hear the man out. He mentions that the dirham pays a better interest rate than the dollar at present. Second, if the U.S. dollar really came under a lot of pressure, he sees an unpegging scenario in which the dirham then pegs to a whole basket. For the meantime, oil is still priced in dollars, but should it be no longer, this currency would move!

The next two he sees as the likely candidates for the world's strongest currency over the next couple years. The key here being a low debt profile.

2. Swedish Krona—this currency is backed by a hawkish central bank, so it's no wonder the euro is turning in multiyear lows against it. The Riksbank, unlike the Swiss, doesn't seem worried about its strength, although some corporations do squawk. It's climbing against the dollar. Its central bankers aren't afraid to hike interest rates.

3. Norwegian Krone—Norway's got some of the biggest budget and current-account surpluses around. Plus, its sovereign wealth fund is pumped full with oil revenues. So Norway's cost to borrow money is very low. It's a coin in very good health.

Commodity-Backed Currencies to Consider

Another petro-backed currency that's pretty strong is the Kuwaiti dinar, but you don't see it exchange hands much outside of the Gulf. Meanwhile, of the other commodity-backed currencies, Canada stands out.

It's been trading stronger than on parity with the U.S. dollar on average for the first time since 1976. We'll also mention it's turned in its strongest performance against the euro since the euro came into existence.

SOLUTION!

Debt-Free and Resource-Rich Currency Baskets

While you can do options on currencies and binaries and a host of other things, you might want to keep it simple.

EverBank puts together a lot of innovative products, especially in the realm of certificates of deposit (CDs) that will reward your saving, by diversifying into currencies around the globe.

Simple favorites are:

World Currency Global Power Shift Basket CD—Focuses on Currencies from Resource-Rich Countries

Australian dollar—25 percent
Brazilian real—25 percent
Canadian dollar—25 percent
Norwegian krone—25 percent

World Currency Debt-Free Basket CD—Hold Currencies from Economies with Little to No Trade Deficit

Australian dollar—20 percent
Brazilian real—20 percent
Japanese yen—20 percent
Singapore dollar—20 percent
Swiss franc—20 percent

But What About the Euro?

Thomas Lapointe, a portfolio manager at Third Avenue, made this crack in his last shareholder letter:

> Once upon a time, as the European Union was being contemplated and before England wisely chose to keep its Pound Sterling (and the right to control its own monetary policy), the saying was, "A successful Euro would have German efficiency, Italian cooking, and British humor; while a failure would feature German humor, Italian efficiency, and British food."

Last time we were writing a book on the dollar, we were actually worried about the competition offered by the euro. It was a big wildcard in our book.

Now, only five years later, the whole experiment is in jeopardy. The differences between the fiscal trajectories of the various Eurozone states are of degree only, not direction. In this game, we'd put our bets that Germany—the last AAA standing—will call the shots. And they could well kick Greece or one of the other paltry PIIGS outta the Union. (The PIIGs being: Portugal, Italy, Ireland, Greece, and Spain).

When our "Daily Reckoning" chief editor Eric Fry took his Farewell Euro tour, he found that plenty of the solid EU nations were ready to stop the bailouts. (Look for the full series on YouTube.) It seems no one in Amsterdam was interested in donating to Eric's PIIGS-Y bank. In fact, according to the word on the street, the whole euro experiment seems like something you regret, like a hangover. And as one shopkeeper put it: "I like more the guilder." Then in Italy, another said that the problem is not the euro, it's the "politica." Naturally, we agree.

There is some measure of sanity that could be applied to troubled euro nations—sell off your national gold pile to meet your bills.

Italy, for instance, currently holds $123 billion in gold (as measured by the current street value). That's more than enough to cover this year's $80 billion budget gap. France has $122 billion of bullion that could make a nice payment on its deficit of $150 billion.

Gold, mind you, is the only currency that no one controls. It knows no party partiality and can't be produced from keystrokes. We expect that China will happily diversify its $3 trillion currency reserves into gold. They'd take payment in that form for sure!

Right now, only Germany, Italy, the Netherlands, and the United States are the big guns on the gold block holding 60 to 80 percent of their reserves in gold.

One thing we'll mention now is this: should any currency decide to back itself with some bullion (before the United States comes to its senses and does so), we'd be in deep doo-doo very fast. Who wouldn't want to fly to that kind of sound promise, in a world of ugly options. Our reserve status would vanish on the double. While this ain't likely, we do mention that in times of crisis, anything becomes possible.

Chapter Eleven

Dollar Apocalypse

The Dollar's Days Are Numbered

WE CAN RUN THROUGH plenty of scenarios and will give some of them down below.

One thing we admit is that the timing will be uncertain. However, we can't dismiss the fact that so many of the experts we interviewed gave the dollar only a decade longer as the world reserve currency.

That was the outside figure—which puts us at 2022.

While we can't pinpoint the year, we can give you a list of the main problems that can and will take out the dollar down the road.

- Reduced foreign investment, signaling we've hit our credit limit.
- Slow foreign demands for U.S. goods continue.
- Unfavorable currency exchange rates damage everything from purchasing power to capital investment.
- Uncle Sam finally can't raise the debt ceiling.
- Inflation heats up beyond the 5 percent level.
- Another nation gold-backs its currency first.
- Oil is no longer priced in dollars.

I'm sure you've heard about the Chinese "nuclear" threat when it comes to our bonds. But here's the thing. We're in such a precarious state that the Chinese don't need to sell our bonds to create untold havoc on our financial system. They just need to stop buying our bonds or just make a serious threat of not buying our bonds.

Keep in mind, too, that should we only keep importing cheap gewgaws and gadgets, but not find markets for our own goods, we'll expand the trade deficit further. A weakening international exchange status for the dollar will only make the situation worse. Forget world travel, dollar attrition can severely cramp U.S. business investment.

We're kidding ourselves if we continue to think that the fate of the U.S. dollar against other currencies is under the control of central banks. The dollar's fate is increasingly held in the hands of millions of fickle investors—who also have their own problems to worry out.

Bailouts may be all the rage now, but what countries can afford to lend a hand, and a cheap borrowing rate, much longer?

Here's how a few of our experts and colleagues see the situation playing out.

China Ends Dollar's Reign

> I tell people at every stop I make that I believe the dollar will lose its reserve currency status in the next 10 years and maybe even sooner. I can point to one country that has its eyes focused on removing the dollar from its lofty perch, and that's China. China's President, Hu, has said that, "the dollar currency system is a product of the past."
>
> —Chuck Butler

China, you see, is taking baby steps. Chuck wagers they're preparing their currency—the yuan—"to ascend to the lofty perch held by the U.S. dollar."

How's that going to happen? They'll start with their trading partners. They'll simply remove dollars from their trade transactions.

It's already happening. They've just signed a currency swap agreement with neighbor Japan. All trade that was dollar-denominated will now be done by exchange of yuan for yen directly.

Thus, each country won't need nearly the stash of dollar reserves they once had. And this isn't the first country to sign a swap agreement cutting out the USD.

China will also exchange directly with Russia, Argentina, Brazil, Belarus, and almost all its Asian neighbors.

Keep in mind, too, there's the fact that China is Africa's largest trading partner. At last count, 13 percent of Sino-African trade is conducted in yuan. But when you're willing to build and finance infrastructure in nations that want to catch up, keep the lights on, and grow economically, deals will be done according to your demands more often than not. That's how China becomes the new financier to the world. Slow and steady.

It will take a few years for China to have its currency ready to float and be more open to investment, but when they do, Chuck says, "the dollar's reign at the top will be over."

Bill Bonner puts the situation more calmly. "The Chinese economy," he agrees "will be the biggest in the world, most likely before 2020." However, he sees a softer scenario for the dollar, a gradual reduction of reserve currency status, which it will share with the yuan and the euro.

Ron Paul: Expects a Basket . . . of Gold

We've had the pleasure of working with Ron Paul on several occasions, and while congressmen really aren't allowed to give investment advice, they can make sound predictions about the general future. (Well, perhaps he's a Cassandra among fools, but we can't think of anyone who better knows the damage Congress has done to the dollar.)

Good Dr. Paul warns:

> But I think eventually the world monetary system will revert to a gold backing. Countries like China, Russia, and the Middle Eastern oil-producing nations understand the importance of gold, the weakness of the dollar, and the necessity of weaning themselves off U.S. debt. If another country were to back its currency by gold, I could see it becoming the preferred reserve currency. I don't think it would happen anytime soon, but the process conceivably could start within the next five to

ten years. The U.S. Congress and Federal Reserve will have only themselves to blame when the U.S. dollar loses its global status.

Naturally, we know Bill Bonner agrees. He calls it Zombie-ism and it's the latest phenomenon he's keeping tabs on in his weekly "Daily Reckoning" essays.

Bill Bonner Lists the Dollar's Three Main Downfalls

1. *Zombie-ism.* Nations decline when their insiders get control of the government and major industries. They pervert the system with privileges, bailouts, subsidies, and so forth. The economy becomes inefficient. And this is a very difficult trap from which to escape. He points out that the remedy typically requires one of two things: a war or a revolution.

2. *Militarism.* Bill applies the concept of zombification to the military, where it is more dangerous. "A man with a gun thinks every problem can be solved by his trigger finger. Look for more spending by the Pentagon, more adventures overseas and more militarization at home. Militarism is profoundly harmful to an economy because it diverts resources from genuine, productive uses."

3. *Bankruptcy*. The Feds are spending too much money. Way too much. They will not be able to cut back. First they will borrow. Then they will print. The result will be catastrophe.

Lawmakers Aren't Ready to Act

Chuck worries that lawmakers won't wield the political will necessary to do something about the debt. So far we've seen no evidence to calm ourselves on that point.

Add to that the fact that housing is still searching for a bottom and many of the jobs lost since 2008 aren't coming back.

While the American consumer—whether unemployed, paying an underwater mortgage, or just battening down the hatches—can actually repair her own balance sheet, it'll probably just be in time for a bout of rising inflation. Chuck calls this our Sword of Damocles.

But lest we give only worries, let's hear some thoughts from our Middle Eastern pal in Dubai, who's not at all as worried as the rest of us.

What the Dollar's Day of Reckoning Will Look Like

Peter Cooper reckons that the dollar's day of reckoning is not going to come until the Eurozone is past its crisis. How long will that take is one question. Will the Eurozone bring the rest of the world down with it in a financial crash? "George Soros certainly thinks so," he admits.

Judging the central banks' abilities to respond, "printing money seems all they can do," Peter suggests. "They all fear the deflationary liquidationist policy of the 1930s and will do anything rather than that."

So he predicts a more extreme version of the 1970s: "a burst of much higher inflation with supermarket trolleys and gas bills hit hard." He also envisions a total bond market bust, as interest rates climb higher out of necessity.

Such a bond climate dooms U.S. domestic policy. The U.S. will then have no alternative but to cut its public spending. The facility to pay for it with borrowed money will be gone. Asset prices will first deflate sharply but then begin to rise again as money from the Fed finds its way into the system.

Eventually the system will be righted with the debt burden eroded by inflation and debt paydowns, and the always latent entrepreneurial genius of the U.S. people will begin to surface with the pressure on the public and not the private sector.

In 30 years' time will the dollar be the global reserve currency? "We think it will survive," Peter declares "because of the absence of a competitor." He does acknowledge that currencies of the emerging markets will be much stronger. Some, he adds, will be depegged from the dollar.

So Peter predicts a slightly softer landing. He certainly doesn't think the euro will come from behind and steal the dollar's crown.

Whatever you make of all this, don't deceive yourself.

The best wool that the feds can pull over your eyes is that they have all this under control. They don't. They've got prejudices and working theories, but remember, there's nothing hard about the "science" of economics.

We didn't want to bore you with the details, and if you remember nothing else from this book, get this one point straight.

If you hear CNBC or Bloomberg declare: "Prices are up 10 percent over the past year" don't just switch off the TV and shrug.

Instead, acknowledge that "last year's dollar is worth 90 cents today" and work on what you can do about it when it comes to your own wallet and your bank account.

The last chapter will round out our solution set, but a huge part of tackling the problem of the shrinking dollar is changing your own mind set.

Change How You Think

Here's where we're at. Ever since the 1990s tech bubble, the world operates as if stock markets were *never* meant to drop. That's the seed of our collapse.

You see, in a healthy society of honest people trading with one another, a financial bubble is painful for some, but ultimately it flushes the system—and gets things back to normal, in the same way that a farmer burns a corn field after a harvest or a forest fire makes new growth jump from the ashes.

After the Fed monkeyed with the interest rate dial after the dot-com crash, bringing benchmark rates down to 1 percent, we didn't get healthy renewal, just a real estate bubble that soon imploded in tandem with the October 2008 market crash.

Now we face the consequences: U.S. dollar decline. Plus, we'll see still more bailouts, outright frauds like MF Global, and plenty more zero interest rates. Thus, those who save for a rainy day will continue to be punished—except if you move your money around right now.

Were these consequences unintended? Well, we won't go all conspiracy theory on you today, but we're not surprised by the acts of the powers that be.

They like to prove that they're needed—by you and by me—it's the only way to grab unprecedented powers, enact legislation that continues to benefit their friends far more than they benefit the average struggling taxpayer who wants to retire happy, and, heck, still loves this country despite the problems it faces.

But there's every reason to end our exploration on a note of optimism. For that we return to the wisdom of Michael Pento and Chris Mayer. At a recent meeting, we overheard them trash-talking the dollar, but here's what they concluded:

MP: Stocks have always risen when currencies flame out. They are claims on real assets, or can be.

CM: Yeah, I'd rather own a piece of a business than leave the money in cash to rot. It is the best shot the average Joe has at making big gains well beyond the inflation rate over a stretch of years.

We also coyly note that the Zimbabwe stock exchange was the best-performing stock exchange across the entire globe in 2007—regarding percentage gains—but not factoring in what the average Zimbabwean lost to inflation. Hence we say again, buy gold. Buy silver. Buy on the corrections. Buy a little a month on an installment plan.

However, we'll add this final word of advice from Chris that rings true: "If you wait around for the monetary system to become rational before you invest, you will die waiting."

Chapter Twelve

Tips on Surviving the Next Crisis

Even More Solutions

THE FED HAS TRIED everything it can to seduce you into buying stocks. But is America taking the bait? This could be an early sign of investors losing faith. Over the first 11 months of 2011, plain-vanilla savings and checking accounts attracted eight times the money that stock and bond mutual and exchange-traded funds did. That's according to data from market research firm TrimTabs.

More money went into bank accounts—even at times when the market rallied. Most recently, investors took $9.35 billion out of equity funds—including more than $7 billion of U.S.-based funds—for the week ending January 4. Should this kind of action escalate, expect the central bank to really panic. Problem is, they're at the end of their rope. They can't cut the interest rate below zero. They can't do anything but more money printing—the exact thing that destroys monetary confidence once and for all.

How bad will it get?

The man who broke the Bank of England in 1992, George Soros is sounding the alarm. While it's not the death knell for the dollar, this billionaire is warning that the current Eurozone crisis holds more danger than 2008.

—————————— ∽ ——————————

"The three biggest challenges to the U.S. economy are the Republicans, the Democrats, and the people who voted for them. They have destroyed the dollar with generations of welfare/warfare spending, and killed the goose that laid the golden egg of American prosperity with their statist economic policies."

—*Charles Goyette, author of* The Dollar Meltdown

In short, it's impossible to gauge how bad things could get. And if you're moving money out of the market for good, don't just stash it under the mattress. Consider farmland. Consider a second home in South America. Do something.

Some of our interviewees were unrepentant pessimists when it comes on how you can act. *The Dollar Meltdown* author Charles Goyette is prepared for total doom.

> No currency today is redeemable in anything other than more of itself. Choosing among them is like asking if you would prefer to sink on the *Lusitania* or the *Titanic*, descending at different rates. Better to man the lifeboats while you can.

We'll offer some more lifeboat investments below, but we only think it's fair to get a slightly less condemning perspective.

Peter Hargreaves, founder of the UK's biggest retail broker doesn't talk about stocks or corporate bonds for his lifeboat. When it comes to fixed-income investment—if and when the euro implodes—he suggests German bonds.

If he had to stash a cool $1 million in cash, he'd split the sum into a $500,000 parcel of Singapore dollars and a $500,000 slug in Norwegian krone.

Ultimately, though, gold is no one's liability, and it knows no foreign borders.

How Would You Like That Gold?

Initially, we thought this was a pretty crazy thing: "Why would someone go to the trouble of stashing gold bars in the 'free zone' at the Zurich airport?"

In 2010, our friend Egon von Greyerz invited me to check out a way station in the global gold bullion trade. Egon has three decades of experience in the global asset–protection business.

We spent nearly a week in Zurich during the European Gold Forum, examining opportunities offered by his firm, Matterhorn Asset Management. Egon gave us a personal tour of the vault facilities and described how one goes about storing gold bars there—outside the reach of even Swiss customs authorities. The vault is used by big banks like UBS to move bullion around the globe for its uber-elite clients, but as Egon showed me, it can be used by individuals quite easily, too. Gold affords you flexibility you can't get otherwise.

For starters, you can keep gold in a safe-deposit box in a foreign bank. Many banks are willing to do this even if you don't have an account. That's because under IRS rules, gold in a safe-deposit box does not qualify as a "foreign financial account."

Sounds great, until you start to think about the logistical hoops you have to jump through to make this happen. You have to buy the gold and then make arrangements for it to arrive at the bank of your choice, where it will then go in the safe deposit box.

That creates its own paper trail. And good luck trying to do it yourself, transporting a significant amount of gold outside the United States.

But there are alternatives that are much easier. In fact, you can take care of it at home, online, in little more than the time it takes to read this report. We call these alternatives OGSPs—"offshore gold savings programs." With them, anyone can have an overseas account.

"People must have physical gold," says Egon. He runs Gold Switzerland, one of three offshore gold savings programs that we've personally vetted. Gold Switzerland stores gold for its clients in massive vaults beneath the Zurich airport.

"I think that they must have it outside of the banking system, and they must have it in their own name," he continues. "They must know that the gold is actually there."

Finding an outfit you trust is what matters most in this case. No matter how much gold you want to store, trust is a big issue if you're going to count on people located on another continent.

Each will store gold for you in "allocated" form—that is, with your name on it, in specialized bullion vaults outside the United States. Your gold won't be mixed up with other people's gold. You own it—the OGSP is merely storing it on your behalf.

The minimum investment if you want access to his vaults beneath the Zurich airport is 125,000 Swiss francs— nearly $140,000. For that kind of sizeable upfront outlay, your commissions are negligible—at most 0.3 percent, if you want your gold in the form of 100-gram bars (a little over 3 ounces).

If your holdings are small by Gold Switzerland's standards, storage costs 2 percent of your total for the first year, 1.75 percent after that. For large holdings of more than 15 million Swiss francs, that fee drops below 1 percent.

If you need to sell your holdings, the commission runs 0.3–0.5 percent. Not surprisingly, given the clientele, Gold Switzerland can make swift, secure, and reasonably priced arrangements if you ever want to move your gold closer to home.

Each OGSP is different, and we encourage you to shop around—this is just a starting point.

Another OGSP, GoldMoney, let's you go digital. James Turk is a 40-year veteran of the precious metals trade, holding positions with Chase Manhattan Bank and the Abu Dhabi Investment Authority, among others, before launching his own research firm in 1985.

And it was with an eye toward gold's re-emergence as money that he launched GoldMoney in 2001, with head-quarters in Jersey, one of Great Britain's Channel Island dependencies.

"I hired a patent attorney in 1992 and filed my first patent application in February 1993. Even then, it was long before the commercial possibilities of the Internet were understood."

Turk's ideal vision of GoldMoney is to have digital gold currency. He did offer a service allowing you to use your GoldMoney account to trade goods and services with the firm's 18,823 customers. For the time being, accounts have gone back to "hold only." The digital gold currency feature," he told *The Gold Report*, "had not been used very actively anyway. In today's world, people would rather spend fiat currency as a form of payment and save their gold and silver."

Indeed, most people take advantage of GoldMoney for the convenience of storing gold in a vault of your choice—London, Zurich, or Hong Kong. Best of all, there's no account minimum. You can start your GoldMoney account with $100 or even less.

Of course, the more you buy, the less you pay in fees. The commission when you purchase is 2.49 percent for amounts under $10,000, falling steadily to 0.99 percent for amounts over $1,000,000.

But no matter how much or how little you buy, GoldMoney arranges it so you won't pay a spread—the premium over the spot price of gold that represents the effort it took to fashion the gold into a coin or a bar. (Go to your neighborhood coin shop and you're lucky if you pay a spread of 6 percent.)

The storage fees are no more than 0.18 percent of your holdings per year. If you choose to sell your holdings at GoldMoney, you pay no commission at all. And if you ever want to take personal possession of your holdings, GoldMoney will work with you on that, too.

Another perennial favorite is BullionVault, headed up by Paul Tustain.

"From postwar Austria to Argentina a decade ago," says Paul Tustain, "it is clear that holding gold bullion offers insurance against many levels of currency crisis—something which a growing number of economic historians think increasingly possible in the developed West today."

With that in mind, he launched London-based Bullion Vault in 2005. He brought with him a quarter-century of experience in both technology and finance. He cut his teeth in London as a stock analyst. Then he launched his own software company, bringing many European banks into the digital age.

Along the way, he acquired an interest in gold and a realization of how hard it was for ordinary people to buy it. "This bothered me," he explains, "because the history is clear: Accessible bullion ownership has regularly provided the essential defense for people who have saved some money and would rather not surrender it to the riskier financial practices which tend to develop over time."

BullionVault gives you a choice of three vaults in which to store your gold—London, Zurich, or New York. (That last choice appeals to non-U.S. customers leery of their own governments, believe it or not.) There is no account minimum.

Buy gold through BullionVault, and you pay a commission of 0.8 percent on the first $30,000. That level falls the more you buy. Spreads are modest. Storage fees are a flat $48 a year on holdings up to $50,000. More than that, and the fee is 0.12 percent of the total. When it comes time to sell, your commission is the same as it is to buy.

BullionVault is not the choice if you're ever looking to take physical delivery—the fees can be quite high.

Another option is to buy coins. There's a lot to learn, especially if you want to get into numismatics. But here's a basic list of simple, good coins (and bars) to hold:

Gold Coins/Gold Bars

1 oz. Canadian Maple Leafs

1 oz. American Eagles

1 oz. American Buffalos

1 oz. South African Krugerrands

1 oz. Vienna Philharmonics

1 oz. Olympic Gold Maples

1 oz. Gold Bullion Bars

100 oz. Gold Bullion Bars

Silver Coins/Silver Bars

1 oz. Canadian Maple Leafs

1 oz. American Eagles

1 oz. Vienna Philharmonics

100 oz. Silver Bullion Bars

Peter Cooper also gave a shout-out to something we've been recommending to readers for years: the Perth Mint.

This is an AAA-rated institution in faraway Western Australia. It is an unallocated gold program that gives you the most bang for your gold buck as there's no commission or storage fee. If you're interested in silver, they've got that too.

A final option comes from innovative EverBank. It offers an easy and affordable solution to owning precious metals. It's called the EverBank Metals select account. For a relatively small amount of cash, you can own a collection of investment-grade precious metal, all securely held at EverBank.

It couldn't be easier. Open a Metals Select account and EverBank will apply your initial deposit to an equivalent amount of gold or silver. There are two types of accounts: allocated and unallocated.

With an allocated account, your initial deposit is applied to coins and bars that you own directly. In fact, you can take actual delivery of your holdings. This type of account has a higher minimum opening balance and some extra fees, including storage.

The unallocated account has no storage fees. Instead, your gold or silver is part of a pool of the precious metals. So you have no control of what goes into that pool, and you cannot choose to have your holdings sent to you. But you can upgrade from an unallocated to an allocated account anytime you want.

As with the currency CDs and money market accounts, the value of your holdings depends on the U.S. dollar. You can convert your holdings to cash anytime you wish. But if the price of gold or silver drops, you will get back less than you paid in the original investment.

You should know that these accounts are not protected by the FDIC. It shouldn't be a problem, however, since EverBank has a long and respected history. And, really, considering the shape of the U.S. government debt, FDIC protection might not be much comfort, anyway.

Is all this really necessary? We know it's a bit of a hassle, but after reading the harrowing story of Marion Szablicki in the November 2011 issue of "Gloom, Boom & Doom," we think a little bit of gold serves anyone well in any kind of crisis.

Mr. Szablicki lived with his wife in eastern Poland in 1939. This time it was not the Germans but the Russians he was afraid of. Poland's great inflation (1923) got Mr. Szablicki wise to gold, which was then the preferred currency. His father taught him: "Gold is the only money that knows no sovereign borders."

In 1940, he was arrested, but because he knew Russian, he was not detained. He went home and lined the bottom of his boots with small coins underneath the insoles. He stuffed gold in the heels, which he'd hollowed out. He stuffed gold chains and coins into his jacket lining.

Just days later, he was awakened by the expected knock. He, his wife, and three-year-old daughter boarded a train to Siberia, never to set foot on Polish soil again. They survived because he had gold to exchange for rubles for bread and food, gold for train passage out of Siberia.

That's why you buy gold; in the hopes that you never need it. You have it, if you do.

Profit from Playing Commodity Catch-Up

> On a global basis we are still living on resource investments made in the 1960s and 1970s. There was a huge dearth of resource related investment in the two decades from 1982 to 2002.
> —Rick Rule, founder of Global Resource Investments,
> an arm of Sprott Asset Management

Juxtapose that with the trends in global population growth. Add in the fact that the emerging markets' desire for Western lifestyles creates a supply/demand imbalance that will last a decade. It's worth getting into natural resources.

There will be unnerving volatility. But the nominal price of these commodities—when denominated in depreciating currencies—should increase dramatically.

Ultimately producer margins and profits will rise. Valuations, says Rule, "will continue to be enhanced by strategic buyers, who buy resource producers to obtain strategic access to resource supplies."

A great example of this we saw at Agora Financial in 2011 was Riversdale Mining. Riversdale sat on a big pile of hard coking coal in Mozambique. Nobody needs high-quality coking coal more than steelmakers, which is why nearly half the company was owned by 'em. China, Brazil, and India's steelmakers all had a strategic interest in getting the riches from Mozambique. They were each eager to score strategic assets for themselves when the time was ripe. Then giant miner Rio Tinto expressed an interest. The bidding war began.

In the end, we didn't wait for the final deal, and took a quick 60 percent gain after holding for less than five months.

Spring for the Picasso?

If ever you want to get out of Dodge in a hurry, and make some quick cash on a hard asset, invest in a painting. Consider the case of Polish Count Jaromir Czernin.

He saw it coming. Count Czernin knew his family's valuable Vermeer was a very worthy asset. Prior to World War II, he was ready to sell. American industry magnate Andrew Mellon was ready to part with $1 million for the thing. That price would have made it the most valuable painting in the world.

There was only one problem. The Austrian government wouldn't allow the Vermeer to leave the country. (See, there's that pesky government again, getting in the way of the free market.) Instead, the situation worsened, both personally and politically.

Soon it was Hitler who wanted the painting. Hitler's private secretary was sniffing out whether back taxes could be used to take the painting away. Meanwhile, envoy Hans Posse offers 1.65 million reichmarks—$660,000. Czernin agreed.

While it's unlikely you'll get your paws on a Vermeer, the ever-popular Picasso was wonderfully prolific—and still holds his value.

According to French research company Artprice, Picasso held the number one rank for world auction prices for all but two years: 2007—when Andy Warhol topped him, and 2011—when Chinese artist Zhang Daqian took the lead.

We asked Dubai-based Peter Cooper whether he'd own a Picasso, over both T-Bills and gold.

"Well," he confesses, "we have just signed up as a guest of Art Dubai in March and would have to choose the Spanish Modern Master.

"It is not that we like Picasso that much as an artist. We toured the Picasso Museum in Barcelona last

November and while his early work is on a par with Leonardo most of the art he produced when he became famous is truly awful."

The factor: scarcity value. When a painter is dead, he may paint no more.

And if the European market is bored, Peter is confident that a Russian oligarch or Brazilian magnate will be ready to buy.

This will raise the eyebrows of many experts in our survey, but Peter called gold "far less certain over time." His reckoning: that from 1980 to 2000 gold was a lousy investment, failing to keep pace with inflation. However he bets 2012 (and beyond) will be a very different period. "We are sure it will perform well as the dollars created over the past three years find their way into the global monetary system."

The nice thing about gold is that you cannot print it. Just like you can't print a Picasso. Peter finishes: "We laugh at the very notion that U.S. Treasuries could be considered a safe long-term asset class."

To Peter, the U.S. Treasury market is likely the biggest investment bubble "of all time." He expects the short-term rally, but discounts that we can ever run from our debts.

"Debt markets always have a tipping point when borrowers require more interest than the debtor can afford and debt is piled on top of debt to pay the interest.

"That has happened in Portugal, Ireland, and, of course Greece. Italy and Spain are teetering on the brink. The dominoes will fall, and, as they do, the glorious isolation of U.S. Treasuries will be exposed as a complete illusion."

Peter points out that nobody "saw through Picasso." He still tops the list of the greatest artists of the twentieth century. But "no such artistic immunity will apply to the bond market."

So back that gold bullion purchase with a Picasso (if you can afford his prices). Eric Sprott agrees. While he'd take a bar of gold "hands down." He says "owning a Picasso probably wouldn't hurt though."

Get Serious about Protecting Your Wealth

Here's the thing. We can give you plenty of solutions, but they're only worth something if you're ready to take the steps necessary to protect and grow your wealth despite the dollar's demise.

The first objective of this book is to be a wake-up call. I'd hope that as soon as you close this book, you'll feel ready to act, to take your finances into your own hands and control your own fate—no matter what Washington might get up to.

Chances are, though, you might be feeling overwhelmed with ideas, and feeling resistant to giving up on the U.S. dollar.

The first thing I suggest you do is come up with a master plan for the next decade. It's simpler than you think.

Chris Martenson, creator of the Crash Course, gives excellent pointers on how to begin acting (even when you feel paralyzed). I'd suggest you check out his website and his book. I owe several of the following tips to him, which I'll apply to the dollar problem.

Seven Steps to Surviving the Next Crisis

1. Take control of your finances: Gauge your exposure to the U.S. dollar.
2. What's your world view?
3. Consider several time horizons: 6 months? 1 year? 5 years? 10 years?
4. Consider whom you're investing for: Yourself? Your parents? Your spouse? Your children?
5. Do I have everything I need in an emergency?
6. Can I move my money at a moment's notice?
7. What do I do first?

1. Take Control of your Finances: Gauge Dollar Exposure

The first thing you need to do is inventory your total exposure to the U.S. economy and the U.S. dollar. Money managers and quants always know this answer, but you should too.

You probably have all of your trading and saving account data on one tidy web page, if you're an active investor. If you're not active, it's time to get involved.

Make a list of all your assets and all your liabilities. Don't forget to list all your property: raw land, houses, condos, and so on. Question each as to how it exposes you to or hedges you against the falling value of the U.S. dollar.

Perhaps you've already diversified into all sorts of international bonds. Perhaps you've got a Swiss account lying idle. Perhaps your spouse has been doing some different things from you. These are all good questions to ask yourself and find answers to.

You get bulky proxy statements in the mail or sent straight to your inbox; read them! Chances are you'll find plenty of surprises on the funds you hold. For example, say you think you're invested in a real estate fund when really the top holdings are companies like Lowe's or retailer Pier One.

Check the fine print. Find out whether your funds can be locked up in event of some market crash or crisis.

2. What's Your World View?

We felt it was our duty to give you a broad working view of the U.S. dollar's decline. Our main takeaway is that you have less than a decade to decide how you want to prepare for a declining U.S. dollar. If you think the facts we presented are unavoidable, you're a dollar bear. If you think that we're over-reading things, or have too little faith in the government, than you're a bull.

Chances are you fall somewhere in between. We suggest getting your feet wet with a few of the simpler moves to hedge yourself, should anything happen. The more comfortable you get, and the more firm your view becomes, the more aggressive you can be.

After all, not everyone is a Jim Rogers type ready to short Treasuries.

3. Consider Several Time Horizons

There's a lot of short-term money to be made as currencies across the world compete and collapse. Consider plays as short as one week or as long as several years.

Create goals for how much of your capital you want to have invested in certain assets by a certain year. Perhaps farmland is your ultimate inflation hedge, but you haven't got the ready money. There'll be a path you can create to deliver the returns you need to get there in 5 or 10 years.

4. Consider Whom You're Investing For

You'll invest differently depending on whom you're caring for. After all, as Rick Rule stressed to us: The young and unborn will be impacted the most by this crisis. Theirs is an inheritance of obligations rather than assets.

You can change that for your kids if you teach them the simple ideas in this book. Starting young really matters.

5. Do I Have Everything I Need in an Emergency?

Find out what information you'll need to make changes—especially in an emergency. I can't stress this enough. Know every account number, phone contact, website, mortgage, and 401(k) or IRA account details. You can keep all the info in one place as long as you store it safely.

6. Can I Move My Money at a Moment's Notice?

Once you've done Step 5, the next step is even more important. Find out what penalties or rules and regulations limit you in any efforts you may make to move your money: 401(k)s might seem straightforward in their penalties, but there could be other surprising terms and conditions you're not aware of. Ask questions like, "If I sold this today, where would the money end up?"

7. What Do I Do First?

Make a trial run. Practice transferring your funds. Place your first currency bet. You can start small—say one move per week—whatever you feel comfortable with.

Hedging a little bit of your money now, and doing too little, is far better than knowing you could have acted and done nothing at all. Ramp up accordingly—especially as you start to see the warning signs we highlighted in Chapter 11.

It's your money. Don't leave chance—or the feds—to wholly determine what it is worth.

Remember, you don't need an offshore account to protect your money. You don't even need to be rich. With this advice, we hope you'll become so.

Feel Like You Don't Know Where to Begin? Start Your Own Investing Group

Use peer pressure to help you achieve all of your dollar-proofing goals.

In 2010, a group of American and Chilean researches followed a group of entrepreneurs. Instead of going it on their own, this group met regularly. They set weekly savings targets, set goals, and discussed failings.

Over the course of the year, the meet-up group socked away twice as much savings as the control group that didn't meet at all. Consider it "keeping up with the Joneses" turned toward positive, proactive goals.

We know the benefits of this kind of community. It's why we've gathered a host of newsletter advisors and top analysts at Agora Financial. You can follow my ongoing advice to get out of the U.S. dollar in my newsletter "Addison Wiggin's Apogee Advisory." And you can join our community by participating in a special lesson-filled, interactive forum called Essential Investor.

I like gold so much that although I am a fairly substantial holder personally, I'd like to see the price go lower, so that I could add to my position. Frankly, in the context of gold being, at least in some measure, a form of catastrophe insurance, I hope the price of gold never rises, and that the events that I fear never occur, but I think the likelihood of that is very low.

—*Rick Rule, Sprott Asset Management*

The "All-Weather" Investment for Today's Shrinking Dollar

One Simple Step to Keep Your Money Safe ... No Matter What

Why are milk, gas and bread prices rising... while your house and flat screen TV prices fall?

The answer lies in "the most important debate of our time."

"Big ticket" items like your house are collapsing under a mountain of debt... while commodities like gasoline are going up — thanks to the printing press run overtime by the Federal Reserve.

In a free report called *The "All-Weather" Investment for Today's Shrinking Dollar,* you can learn the simple step you can take to keep your money safe regardless of which way the economy goes.

Get your free copy by visiting:
http://agorafinancial.com/shrinkingdollar

Regards,

Addison

P.S. Remember, go to **http://agorafinancial.com/shrinkingdollar** and get our latest report on this one simple step you can take to keep your money safe...no matter what.